MATERIAL ALCHEMY

By

STUDIO AIKIEU

BIS

BIS Publishers
Building Het Sieraad
Postjesweg 1
1057 DT Amsterdam
The Netherlands
T +31 (0)20 515 02 30
F +31 (0)20 515 02 39
bis@bispublishers.nl
www.bispublishers.nl

ISBN 978 90 6369 376 3

Editor: Jenny Lee
Front Cover Design: Studio Aikieu & Jennifer Moors

Font: Ostrich Sans by Tyler Finck, Calibri by Microsoft.

Music: "Candlepower" by Chris Zabriskie. Available on the Free Music Archive http://freemusicarchive.org. Under CC BY Attribution License http://creativecommons.org/licenses/by/4.0/

Publishing Information

ACKNOWLEDGEMENTS

I would like to express my deepest appreciation and gratitude to those who have supported my ideas and made this publication a success. Without their continuous support and dedication, this publication would not exist today.

I would like to thank Rowan Bailey and Clair Sweeney for their meticulous attention to detail and in taking the time to cast their critical eye over the publication. To my family friend Peter Kingsnorth for his technical expertise, advice and support.

Many thanks to the alchemists who provided key insight to material developments within the 21st century and to all the workshop contributors that have kindly donated their workshop plans to enable our readers the chance to explore and interact with materials in a playful and innovative manner.

I would also like to thank the team for their enormous contribution to the book. For, without their technical expertise, extensive knowledge and shared vision the book would not be as rich and compelling.

Thomas Forth and the imactive team, for their contribution in the creation of the app, which has provided an additional creative dimension to the publication and Josie Capel for her hardwork and commitment in creating interactive content.

Philippa Wagner and Unique Style Platform for their knowledge and expertise in material forecasting and Laura Martinez for her incredible retouching skills.

Finally, to my partner Daniel Loader, who gave me the courage to take risks and the confidence to believe in myself.

THE VISION

LOW-TECH

MOLECULAR GASTRONOMY

Contents

Material Alchemy

FOREWORD

Material Alchemy

Materials are having a moment. Simply, they define a shape, a texture, a pattern, a mood, a function and a provenance. Of course materials in themselves are not new, they make up objects, products, clothing and buildings around us, but what is different is that materials are no longer simply about mere ingredients or an after-thought to a design and function. Materials are getting clever, unexpected and overly functional.

The materials palette that we have to dip into is also rapidly shifting and moving. For a fashion designer, previously it was a limited palette made up of wool, silk, cotton, leather etc., but in recent years, with the advent of rapid prototyping, we are seeing designers, notably Iris Van Herpen and Neri Oxman, create garments in collaboration with architects and engineers, scoping out materials in entirely new dimensions.

We also see the future of textile production being turned on its head with the advancements of synthetic biology and protocells, whereby strawberry plants of the future could also harvest lace and synthetic materials can morph and shape according to function, as outlined in the project of Shamees Aden.

Projects pioneered by the likes of Suzanne Lee and her Biocouture have generated a series of spin off projects all exploring how we can 'grow' materials in the future - but not in the traditional sense - turning our perception of materials on its head and changing the way that we interact with materials today and in the future.

It is in the meeting of the minds between technology and nature where the most interesting shifts are occurring in materials. More than a sustainable drive, we are seeing how materials are being re-purposed in new ways as virgin materials are being depleted. More notably it is in the cross fertilisation of materials where a new breed of designers are evolving. These materiologists, as I first named them a few years ago, are those designers who are non descript in as much that they are happy to cross boundaries, explore the unexplored and are driven by materiality.

True materiologists, epitomising how materials, nature and technology fuse, are design duo Thomas Vailly and Laura Lynn Jansen with their CaCO3 - Stoneware project. Working in a cross disciplinary manner with scientists, geologists and craftsmen they have crafted future fossils by using nature's geological strengths partnered with modern material engineering via 3D printing. The way they approach materiality through design highlights the future of materials, as does the work of Sophie Rowley, who is imagining a materials future whereby man-made materials synthesise themselves

Material Illusions by Sophie Rowley, photography by Emilie Flood

into future naturals. Interestingly, our aesthetics of materials is also changing.

In a recent design research project Merel Bekking used an MRI scanner to determine preferred materials and colour vs information gathered by a simple questionnaire. When asked, participants overwhelmingly stated that natural materials were their favourite, but when shown images whilst their brains were being scanned, plastic and red caused more positive responses suggesting that our choices and likes in materials are shifting.

What we perhaps once perceived as cheap and nasty is now taking on a new role as more luxurious or perhaps the norm. In the same way that materials were assumed as inanimate, we now don't question (and in some cases) expect them to morph and adapt. With the advent of nanotechnology it is not entirely inconceivable for us,

The Vision: Foreword by Philippa Wagner

Material Alchemy

in the near future, to be able to have materials that change colour and shape shift. Materials are the Holy Grail, but as advances in nanotechnology evolve it is not entirely outlandish to begin to imagine how materials will evolve.

But more than smart, materials are fundamental to everything we engage with, be it food, our clothing or the touch of our smart phone screens. They are what we surround ourselves with – the ingredients of our everyday lives.

Philippa Wagner is a materials and innovation consultant who explores our material futures. Tracking trends and technology she is an authority on materiality and design futures.

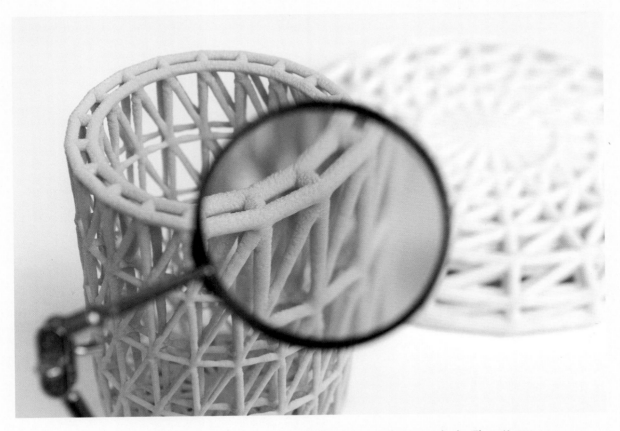

CaCO3 Stoneware by Thomas Vailly & Laura Lynn Jansen, photography by Floor Knaapen

INTRODUCTION

Material Alchemy

Over the last ten years there has been a huge growth in materials for design; key global issues such as the decline in natural resources, a growing and ageing population, recession, and changes in our economic and environmental climate, has led designers and scientists to consider future trends that may emerge, and how we may design for a more sustainable future.

Austerity

In 2008 unemployment increased and poverty also hit an all time high. With government cuts, inflation rising and food and energy prices soaring, we saw a significant shift in consumer spending. The recession triggered a response in consumers to re-evaluate their lifestyles, leading to a shift in behaviour and the rediscovery of core values, placing relationships and experiences above material things (Kadlec, 2013). The throwaway culture declined, with consumers wanting more from their products, emphasising the need for personality, creative expression and emotional value.

During this period we saw a rise in depression and health related issues, leading designers to focus on more poignant themes such as heritage and craftsmanship to bring back a sense of value, meaning and narrative into products.

Poor Tools by Studio Fludd takes on a playful approach in the celebration of overlooked, discarded materials. Crafting a set of intriguing artefacts, that combines the natural with the artificial, they convey the story of the wild and chaotic landscape of La Certosa. Poor Tools highlights the importance of imagination and narrative in an over saturated society, where design becomes omnipresent due to the abundance of objects that surround us.

Chris Lefteri (2014) argues, *"Materials are increasingly becoming central characters in consumer focused stories"*.

Our desire for intrinsic value and connectedness has driven the way for new interpretations of materiality, as opposed to merely applying materials as an afterthought (Lefteri, 2014). The Chapter 'Material Narratives' showcases the works of extraordinary materiologists and artisans, who approach materiality in unconventional ways. Rituals, narrative and imagination play a key role in the development of tangible materials, bridging the gap between value and aesthetics.

Post Scarcity

The age of austerity has led to the growth of synthetic materials in the form of synthetic biology. It has been predicted that by 2060 the human population will rise to 9.5 billion (Jha, 2013), leading to a growing demand for materials such as food, fuel and clothing.

Professor Mark Post from Maastricht University has produced the very first in-vitro meat, which is set to change the face of food production, dramatically reducing the need for land and water by 90% and cutting overall energy use by 70% (Jha, 2013). Synthetic meat may be the answer to our growing demand, and potentially be an environmental, even ethical, solution.

A recent exhibition held at Dublin Science Gallery entitled Grow your Own, curated by Alexandra Daisy Ginsberg, showcases ground-breaking and thought-provoking work by designers and scientists who are designing with living matter. The exhibition demonstrates how designers are utilising the laboratory as a means to cultivate and grow new materials. They seek to harness living organisms to produce anything from fuel to clothing. With the potential synthetic biology could hold for the future, there is much to consider:

"Re-imagining biology — and life with it — into fully engineerable and designable material is no small matter, technical or ethically. We may be undertaking the biggest engineering project man has applied to nature yet" (Ginsberg, 2013).

Within this publication, the chapters 'The Laboratory' and 'Material Appropriation' examine the potential of synthetic biology in greater detail. Body Architect Lucy McRae's project Make your Maker examines genetic manipulation and human cloning,

"delivering a world where clones are edible; their sensory effects absorbed through the body" (McRae, 2014).

The works of design studio The Kitchen by Amy Congdon and JJ Hastings, seek to explore the scientific technique 'decellularising', a process which removes the cells from organs, leaving the remains of the extracellular matrix, which can then be cultivated as a new material, leading us to question what our material future might be?

Design Ecology

With a shift in consumer behaviour and attitudes, consumers are becoming more discerning with what they purchase and why. This change in attitude is a response to the Anthropocene: The Age of Man. Anthropocene is a term used by geologists to describe the impact humanity's ecological footprint is having on the Earth's ecosystem. The most notable effects of the Anthropocene are changes in weather patterns, providing tangible evidence of the impact our carbon footprint is having on our environment.

In 2011 the Geological Society of America held an annual meeting called Archean to Anthropocene: The Past is the Key to the Future. The conference brought together government, academics, researchers and educators to exchange knowledge and ideas to examine how we may find ecological solutions to reduce the impact of human activities.

The Vision: Introduction by Studio Aikieu

Material Alchemy

In response to this, designers are exploring unconventional materials and methods of production. The chapter 'Material Interaction' showcases the work of Arabeschi di Latte's project The Archeo Mill; a conceptual factory that enables designers to reclaim control over the manufacturing process, whilst encouraging consumers to participate in the production process, re-establishing an intrinsic relationship between maker and consumer. Consequently, it provides not only a more meaningful product, but also one that confronts issues concerning industrialisation, production and consumption.

The chapter 'Material Provenance' presents the work of designers who seek to examine the past to design for the future. Design Duo Formafantasma presents De Natura Fossilium; a critical investigation that seeks to examine the relationship between tradition and local culture. This project highlights the need to revive lost processes and materials, in the attempt to design for a more sustainable future.

Playful Interactions

Material Alchemy has been devised to showcase the most innovative, thought-provoking design approaches to materials within the 21st century. Enlisting the help of luminaries from the world of science, technology, and design showcases new responses to material innovation and provides key insights into how materials will be utilised to shape our future environments.

Unlike existing publications that singularly examine and showcase materials from an industrial and technical standpoint for commercial application, this publication explores materials from a conceptual, historical and narrative point of view.

It not only provides new insights into how designers, scientists and artisans are exploring materiality, it also presents opportunities to physically engage with materials through the following chapters: 'Low-Tech', 'High-Tech', 'Molecular Gastronomy' and 'The Laboratory'.

Merging the Analogue with the Digital

In addition to this, we have collaborated with a digital producer to create an interactive publication that merges the analogue with the digital. Downloading the free app, will allow you to scan the pages to trigger additional information such as animations that visually demonstrate how to carry out each workshop and to transport you to a designer's conceptual film to further explain the narrative of their research.

We hope that you find this book useful and inspiring, and that it will rouse a sense of curiosity and wonderment in your journey of material discovery.

Jenny Lee
Studio Aikieu

How to download the App for Apple Devices

1. Click on the App Store Icon

2. Click on the Search Icon

3. Type in Material Alchemy

4. Click on Material Alchemy App

5. Click on the Free Icon

6. Click on the Install Icon

7. Enter your iTunes password

8. This will now download

9. Once downloaded it is ready to use

The Vision: How to Use the Book

Material Alchemy

How to download the
App for Android™ Devices

1. Click on the Google Play Store™ Icon

2. Click on the Search Icon

Material Alchemy ✕

3. Type in Material Alchemy

4. Click on Material Alchemy App

Download

5. Click on the Download Icon

Accept & Download

6. Click on the Accept & Download Icon

7. App will install and download

8. Click to open the app when the option appears

9. App can also be accessed from the App Drawer

Using the App

1. Open the App
Click on the App to open.

2. Image Recognition Mode
Hover your phone/tablet over an image in the book to trigger hidden content.

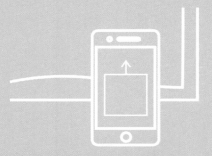

3. Trigger the Animation
The app will recognise the image which will trigger the animation to play.

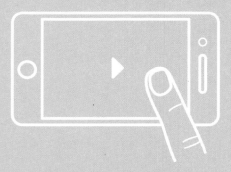

4. Pause/Play
Tap on the screen to pause or play the animation.

The Vision: How to Use the Book

Using the App

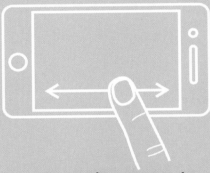

5. Rewind/Fast-Forward
Swipe across the screen to rewind or fast-forward.

6. IR Mode
To access the IR mode to rescan the pages.

7. Contributor
Learn more about the contributor.

8. Camera Icon
To access the camera mode to takes photographs.

MATERIAL
FORECASTING

Material Alchemy

Materials are increasingly taking centre stage in the design and function of new products. In the fashion industry, in particular, garments are more defined by the fabrics they use than ever before, meaning that understanding materials has never been more relevant.

The trend forecasting world has a vested interest in the evolution of materials, as they play a growing role in the $1.5 trillion fashion industry, as well as adjacent categories like tech, automotive, hospitality, retail, food, beauty and interiors. For the style-seekers, analysts, designers and experts that make up the $60 billion trend forecasting industry, material innovation is a useful indicator of the future possibilities of design and production.

Materials are one of the first, and most defining elements in the creation of a product, impacting design, sourcing and manufacturing. Particularly in fashion, material types and usage evolve from one season to the next and the processes and techniques used to create brushed or high-shine textures vary. At the same time, yarns sway from synthetic to natural to blends. Shifts in materials can be incremental (like easy-care coatings) or seismic (like the introduction of Lycra®) but they increasingly define a fashion season as much as a certain colour or silhouette ever did.

It is not just in the fashion arena that materials in themselves are defining a product, materials also impact functionality as well aesthetically. As such, trends in lifestyle and materials have become intrinsic to the way that designers explore the narratives that inform design.

Tracking material trends and evolutions, USP's material directions for autumn/winter are defined by the intersection of nature and innovation, as luxury shifts towards the fundamental, organics go scientific and unconventional materials offer a new and engaging tactility.

ODDCORE

ENABLED BY TECHNOLOGY, INNOVATORS ARE CREATING THE
UNIMAGINABLE AND PUSHING THE BOUNDARIES OF DESIGN.
USING ALL THE SENSES ENGAGES CONSUMERS ON NEW LEVELS,
AS COLOUR AND TEXTURE ARE LAYERED AND DISTORTED TO
EMBRACE A NEW 4D DIGITAL AESTHETIC.

AS WE REASSESS WHAT IT IS TO BE 'NORMAL', STEREOTYPES
ARE REDEFINED, CREATING A VISIONARY FUTURE AND DYNAMIC,
SURPRISING MATERIALS.

USING LIGHT ON TRANSPARENT AND REFLECTIVE SURFACES,
AS SEEN IN PHOTOGRAPHY, FASHION AND PRODUCT DESIGN,
CREATES DYNAMIC AND FUTURISTIC COMBINATIONS.
MATERIALS AND SURFACES OSCILLATE BETWEEN THE
SYNTHETICALLY FANTASTICAL TO THE UTTERLY ORDINARY,
ALL VIBRATE WITH INTENSITY AND TACTILITY.

Material Forecasting by Unique Style Platform

Material Alchemy

KEY WORDS:
LAYERED +
VISIONARY + DYNAMIC +
SURPRISING + AUGMENTED + VIVID

KEY WORDS

RUDIMENTARY+
PURE + SENSORY +
RECLAIMED + TACTILE + FUNDAMENTAL

Material Forecasting by Unique Style Platform

Material Alchemy

HONEST

FINDING BEAUTY IN IMPERFECTION AND VALUE IN THE
FORGOTTEN INSPIRES A HISTORICAL JOURNEY THROUGH
MATERIALS.

INTRODUCING AN ELEMENT OF SURPRISE AROUND ORDINARY
OBJECTS CREATES EMOTIVE, TACTILE EXPERIENCES WITH
PREVIOUSLY OVERLOOKED MATERIALS.

RAW LUXURY IS DEFINED BY TIME, EMOTION AND THE SENSES,
WHILE METAL, WOOD, BONE AND STONE CREATE A NEW TAKE
ON INDULGENT BASICS.

INTERPLAYING IDEAS OF LUXURY WITH THE
UNDERAPPRECIATED CREATES A NEW SENSE OF VALUE.
MATERIAL QUALITIES ARE SOFTLY TACTILE, WITH NATURAL
GRAINS AND IMPERFECTIONS ADDING RESONANCE.

CREATIFICATION

THE URBAN LANDSCAPE IS REDEFINED WITH RURAL SENSIBILITIES. DIY MAKER CULTURE INTERWEAVES RUDIMENTARY MATERIALS COMBINED WITH INNOVATIVE TECHNOLOGY, INSPIRING MATERIALS MERGE SCIENCE AND NATURE FOR A NEW TAKE ON CONTEMPORARY CRAFT.

3D PRINTING AND BIOPLASTICS ARE INFLUENCED BY THE SKINS OF FRUITS AND VEGETABLES, AS THE ORGANIC AND INVENTIVE EXIST CHEEK-BY-JOWL.

FOOD CULTURE GETS MORE PROGRESSIVE, WITH CONSUMERS, DESIGNERS, SCIENTISTS, CHEFS AND FARMERS SEARCHING FOR ALTERNATIVE WAYS TO NURTURE BODY AND SOUL.

FLUCTUATING BETWEEN NATURAL AND MAN-MADE, THESE MATERIALS ARE CARVING OUT A NEW PLACE IN THE TEXTURAL PALETTE. BIOPLASTICS SHIFT OUR PERCEPTIONS OF TOUCH, WHILE SYNTHETICALLY ENGINEERED PLANTS TAKE ON A NEW LUSHNESS. NATURAL MIMICS SYNTHETIC AND VICE VERSA IN A SENSITIVE INTERMINGLING OF TACTILITY.

1 gelb/yellow
jaune
32g 130°C/265°F D0

KEY WORDS

HAPTIC +
BALANCED + NOURISH +
HANDMADE + ORIGINAL + SCIENTIFIC

THEMES

TRACKING AND IDENTIFYING KEY OVERARCHING THEMES IN MATERIALS, BIG THINKING IDEAS ARE DRIVING TRENDS, WITH INNOVATION, PURPOSE AND THE ENVIRONMENT UNDERPINNING ONGOING MATERIAL DEVELOPMENTS. THE CURRENT GENERATION OF MATERIAL ALCHEMISTS ARE FINDING NEW WAYS TO CREATE FABRICS THAT OFFER GREATER FUNCTION AS WELL AS MATERIALS THAT ANSWER ISSUES OF WASTE, FOOD POVERTY AND GLOBAL LIFESTYLES. WITH GROWING AWARENESS OF THE IMPACT OF MATERIALS ON THE ENVIRONMENT, MATERIAL LIFECYCLES AND ECOCONSCIOUSNESS ARE AT THE CORE OF FUTURE MATERIALS.

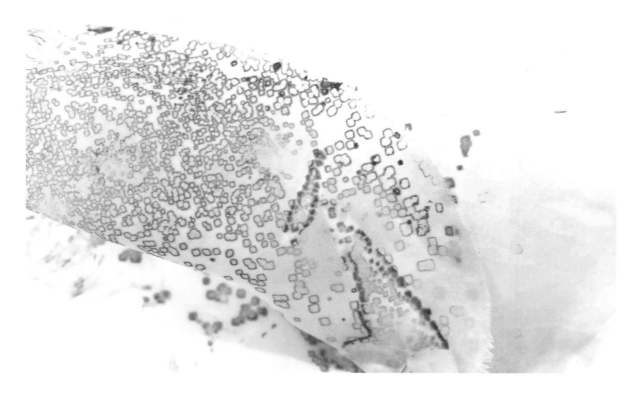

Faber Futures by Natsai Chieza

Material Forecasting by Unique Style Platform

SUPER

At a time of scientific mastery, designers and scientists are collaborating to craft the living. Synthetic manufacture is an ongoing theme for material visionaries: rather than growing crops of cotton or flax, designers are proposing ways to grow materials through innovative biology. Carole Collet's Biolace concept aims to produce enough food and textiles for future populations, by genetically engineering strawberry plants to grow lace-like roots. Meanwhile, the 'biofacture' movement is using bacteria, algae, cellulose and protein to create alternative fabrics. Natsai Audrey Chieza's project Faber Futures uses dyes created by bioengineered bacteria for traditional screen-printing techniques, while Zuzana Gombosova has created a machine that controls the growth of bacterial cellulose and 'prints' organic matter. Suzanne Lee, founder of Biocouture, brings live and biological materials to the fashion industry, creating fabrics by brewing bacteria in a similar way to beer. More than sustainability this area of materials research and exploration is underpinned by a need to evolve a new genre of materials befitting a synthetically sustainable future.

SYNTHETICS

ADAPTIVE

As the fashion industry becomes increasingly global, it demands fabrics that work across different seasons and climates. Winter no longer requires the heavy wools and felting associated with northern climes, while summer's lightness and brevity must adapt to more modest markets. As a result, designers are increasingly creating materials that can adapt to changing seasons.

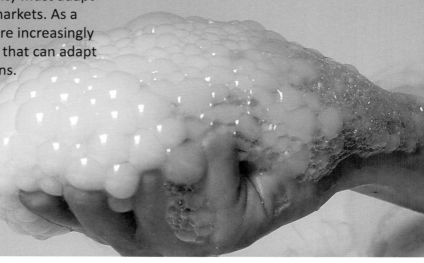

Wondermaterials by Clemens Winkler

Fabrics developed for active wear, with breathable or sweat wicking properties are increasingly being adopted by mainstream fashion, such as Uniqlo's HeatTech line.

Material Alchemy

Amoeba Trainer by Shamees Aden,
photography by Sam J Bond

With increasing fabric technology, materials may be getting denser, but they are also more lightweight and more adaptable. Phase-change materials can adapt to temperature thanks to microcapsules that are embedded in the textile which give off heat, when in a solid state, or absorb heat as they turn liquid. As these technologies go mainstream, the next evolution of phase-change materials will bring even greater change. Nanocoatings and nanobots, for example, offer a futuristic – but not unrealistic – vision for materials. More than wearable electronics (like Google Glasses and Nike's Fuelband), these enhanced textiles will harvest energy during exercise or self-clean, thanks to nanobots that can reconfigure themselves and their material makeup. These kinds of smart textiles are gaining increasing attention from the generation of 'digital natives', who expect their clothing and material objects to have high-tech attributes.

MATERIALS

MAN-MADE NATURE

Virgin materials are increasingly rare, expensive and problematic to produce, leading many designers to repurpose existing materials. While the environmental waste of growing and dyeing natural materials (it takes 20,000 litres of water to grow 1 kilogram of cotton) plays its part, this shift is more than environmental. It takes the possibilities from innovative materials and adapts them to forgotten, surplus or waste objects to create something entirely new.

From Insects by Marlene Huissoud

Material Forecasting by Unique Style Platform

Material Alchemy

UK   LONDON   CHELSEA

Dust Matters by Lucie Libotte

South Korean designer Jeongwon Ji has created a bioplastic from a glucose found in the shells of the invasive mitten crab species, making the crustacean menace a more useful species, while Lucie Libotte repurposes household dust into ceramic glazes, and Marlene Huissoud turns propolis – a waste created in beehives – into a resin-like material. It is not just designers who are repurposing waste materials – the earth's ecosystem is creating nature from the synthetic. Scientists have discovered a form of rock created from waste plastic, which they have dubbed 'plastiglomerate', and may be evidence of the planet beginning to create nature from the man-made. This breed of material alchemists are paving the way for a new materials palette that is yet to exist. Sitting somewhere between the plausible and implausible, they are redefining what we consider materials to be.

LOW-TECH

Material Alchemy

Living in a digital age where technology has become the main focus for design solutions and progressive socioevolution, we see a new form of craft emerge.

Designers are going back to basics, revisiting simple, unsophisticated technologies that spark our inventiveness, turning humble ideas into ingenious creations.

Organisations and designers have revolutionised the way we perceive and utilise materials. For example, Bare Conductive are an organisation formed from a collaborative student project between the Royal College of Art and Imperial College London.

Their aim was to develop accessible platforms to enable anyone of any age to engage with technology in a low-tech creative way, making learning intuitive and fun.

This area explores low-tech methods and materials that encourage playful interactions, to stimulate creativity, enabling the end user to tinker, design and build their own devices and realise the potential of their imagination.

It follows the Makers Movement by actively encouraging individuals to learn through the process of making.

INGREDIENTS

1 cup of Water
1 cup of Flour
¼ cup of Salt
3 tbsp of Cream of Tartar
1 tbsp of Vegetable Oil
Couple of drops of Food
Colouring
1 x LED
1 x 9 volt Battery

EQUIPMENT

Measuring Cups
Non-Stick Pan
Spatula

HEALTH & SAFETY

Take care when working with heat, materials will be extremely hot.

OTHER INFORMATION

See technical data section for circuit diagram.

See suppliers section for where to purchase materials.

Visit University of St Thomas's website for more workshops and information.

HOW TO GUIDE

1. Measure out your ingredients.
2. Mix all the ingredients together in the pan.
3. Continue to stir the ingredients over a medium heat (do not burn. The mixture will begin to boil and start getting chunky).
4. Keep stirring the mixture until it forms a ball in the centre of the pot.
5. Once a ball forms, place the ball on a lightly floured surface (Be careful when handling the dough it will be extremely hot).
6. Flatten the ball to let it cool.
7. Slowly knead the remaining flour into the ball until you have reached the right dough consistency.
8. You are now ready to use it!
9. Test the conductivity of the dough by creating a squishy circuit (see technical section for circuit diagram if you are a complete novice to electronics). This is where your creativity comes in – can you think outside of the box?
10. Store the ball in an airtight container until you are ready to use it. This should last several weeks if stored well.

Low-Tech: Squishy Circuits by Dr. AnnMarie Thomas & the Playful Learning Lab

Material Alchemy

INGREDIENTS

Bare Conductive Paint
350gsm Paper
1 x 555 Timer
1 x Breadboard
1 x Battery Clip & 9v Battery
1 x LED
10 x Jumper Wires
1 x 330 ohm Resistor
2 x 2.7 mega ohm Resistor
1 x 10nF Capacitor
4 x Paper Clips

EQUIPMENT

Paint Brush
Solder
Soldering Iron

HEALTH & SAFETY

Take care when working with a soldering iron, it gets very hot. Never cut a cable that goes directly to a mains power.

OTHER INFORMATION

See technical data section for further information about Bare Conductive ink and diagrams for this workshop.

Visit Bare Conductive's website to purchase the kit and for more workshops and information.

CAN YOU HACK IT?

This workshop is relatively easy and requires no coding. However, with electronics, things are not always straightforward, so a great deal of care and attention to detail is required when assembling the circuit. We have simplified the workshop but it is worth considering working with someone who has some knowledge of electronics. Don't forget that there are many open source platforms with helpful forums should you need support.

Low-Tech: Touch Sensitive by Bare Conductive

Material Alchemy

HOW TO GUIDE

CONDUCTIVE INK

1. Draw your diagram with conductive ink, leave to dry.

555 TIMER

2. The 555 Timer has 8 legs that needs to be connected (see diagram).
3. Connect the Timer to the breadboard (leg 1 in slot G11 and leg 8 in slot F11).
4. Leg 1: Connect a wire from leg 1 (slot L11) to Ground (black row) on the breadboard.
5. Leg 2: Connect a 2.7M ohm resistor (A) to Leg 2 (slot K9 & K12).
6. Leg 3: Connect positive leg of LED to Leg 3 (slot J13) and the negative leg to slot J17.
7. Leg 4 and 8: Connect a wire from leg 4 (slot H14) to leg 8 (slot E11).
8. Leg 5: Connect a capacitor to leg 5 (slot D14 & slot D18).
9. Leg 6: Connect a 2.7M ohm resistor (B) to leg 6 (slot C13 & slot C6).
10. Leg 7 has no connection.

11. Leg 8: Connect a wire from leg 8 from slot A11 to Live (red row) on the breadboard.
12. LED: Connect a 330 ohm resistor from slot L17 to Ground (black row).
13. Capacitor: Connect a wire from slot E18 to Ground (black row).
14. 2.7M ohm Resistor (B): Connect a wire from slot E6 to Ground (black row).
15. Connect a wire from slot 14 and slot 17 on Live (red row).

TOUCH BUTTONS

16. Solder a paper clip to the end of each jumper wire.
17. ON Button: Connect a jumper wire from Ground (slot 1).
18. ON Button: Connect a jumper wire from slot L12.
19. OFF Button: Connect a jumper wire from Live (red row) (slot 1).
20. OFF Button: Connect a jumper wire from slot A13.

BATTERY

21. Connect the black wire to Ground (slot 30).
22. Connect the red wire to Live (slot 30).
23. Connect the battery.

Low-Tech: Touch Sensitive by Bare Conductive

24. Fix each paper clip to the corresponding button on the paper.
25. Touch your paper buttons to turn the LED on and off.

TIPS

26. If your touch sensitive circuit doesn't work, double check that the components are in the correct place and also double check that the components themselves are working.
27. If the LED turns on but the touch buttons don't work correctly, it may be that the 555 timer has burnt out, therefore you will need to replace this.

INGREDIENTS

Graphite Pencils in different grades
Paper
1x Signal Generator Kit MK105 (Velleman)
1x 9 volt Battery
1 pair of Speakers
Crocodile Clips
1x 2 meters of Bell Wire
1x 2-Pin Wire Connector & Plug

EQUIPMENT

Multimeter
Soldering Iron
Solder
Soldering Stand
Wire Cutter

HEALTH & SAFETY

Take care when working with a soldering iron, it gets very hot. Never cut a cable that goes directly to a mains power. If you modify the cable of the loudspeakers, make sure to use the audio cable as shown in the technical section. Carry out this work only with a specialist.

OTHER INFORMATION

See technical data section for further information about graphite and for the lab sheets.

See suppliers section for where to purchase materials.

Visit Berit's website for more workshops and information.

CAN YOU HACK IT?

This workshop is relatively easy and requires no coding. However, with electronics, things are not always straightforward, so a great deal of care and attention to detail is required when assembling the circuit. We have simplified the workshop but it is worth considering working with someone who has some knowledge of electronics. Don't forget that there are many open source platforms with helpful forums should you need support.

Low-Tech: Graphite Sounds by Berit Greinke

HOW TO GUIDE

ASSEMBLING THE ELECTRONICS

1. Assemble and solder the Signal Generator circuit according to the manual. Leave out the resistor R7.
2. Cut your bell wire into four lengths (label a, b, c, d).
3. Solder bell wire (a and b) to each end of the R7 position on the Circuit Board.
4. Fix the other end of bell wire (a and b) in the socket of the 2-pin wire connector.
5. Solder the plug on the 2-pin wire connector to the other two bell wire (c and d) and stabilise the ends with some solder or by forming a loop.
6. Connect the 2-pin wire to the plug.
7. Insert the battery in the holder.
8. Connect Crocodile Clip A (red) to the out pin on the circuit board.
9. Connect the Crocodile Clip B (black) to the Ground (GND) pin on the circuit board.
10. Connect your circuit board to the speaker cable with crocodile clips. Connect Crocodile Clip B (black) to the bottom of the Jack (metal tip) and Crocodile Clip A (red) to the top of the Jack.

PREPARING THE GRAPHITE LAB SHEETS

11. Prepare lab sheets to test the conductivity of your drawings. A lab sheet contains a shape, which can be repeatedly drawn with different graphite utensils, applying more or less pressure while drawing or varying the number of layers. The easiest would be to start with simple lines and rectangles.

12. Use your drawing tools to fill the shapes, making sure that all shapes have roughly the same size. This is the part where your individual drawing techniques will make all the difference, and there is no right or wrong! Your drawings can be technical and organised, or chaotic and diffused. How your drawing looks will depend on your preferred method and the drawing tool you are using.

13. Within a series of test drawings, you should use the same method and the same tool. Make sure to take a note of how each drawing is done. This will help you to identify and remember

Low-Tech: Graphite Sounds by Berit Greinke

the method that you want to use in your final drawing.

14. You can use the multimeter to measure the electrical resistance of your drawings. (This part isn't necessary). Turn the multimeter to the ohms section. Choose two points at the outer ends of your drawings, and try to always keep a similar location when measuring. Take a note of each result.

MAKE GRAPHITE SOUNDS

15. Now use the Signal Generator circuit to listen to your test drawings. Hold the two wires coming from resistor R7 on either end of your graphite drawing. Switch on the loudspeakers and adjust the volume level. You can also use the potentiometer on the circuit board for that. This should now make sounds.

16. You have now established a system for making sound drawings, using your favourite drawing tools and methods. Some of these results will help you in the next step: Create a beautiful drawing that makes exactly the sound you would like it to make. Check the sound of your drawing frequently while you are creating it. You can even produce a chord by making three signal generator circuits and creating three harmonic graphite drawings as a series!

USEFUL TIPS

17. Drawings are simple resistors and can be used in many different types of circuits. This workshop can be as simple as changing the brightness of an LED, or disassembling and pimping an entire 1970's analogue synthesiser to create new eerie sound effects.

18. If your graphite sound system doesn't work there could be several reasons for this:

- You have assembled the electronics incorrectly.
- You have a loose connection somewhere in the electronics.
- There isn't enough graphite to create a sound.

MOLECULAR
GASTRONOMY

Material Alchemy

The use of kitchen ingredients to fashion unimaginable materials is becoming mainstream, due to the rise in demand for more sustainable products that minimise waste and reduces the impact on our future environments.

Inspired by the likes of Heston Blumenthal for his experimental approach to food, whereby he imagines ingredients, as scientific substances that can be cultivated to his will, he uses precise, scientific methodologies to enhance the flavours and textures of food through the modification of their molecule structures.

Materiologists such as Emily Crane seek to cultivate new experiences in a throw away society. Her project Micro Nutrient Couture explores the transient nature of fashion, cooking up new materials that provide the wearer with the opportunity to create biodegradable one-off fashion pieces. In her high-tech kitchen, she devises new processes that consider the environmental impact of current fashion cycles on our future environment.

"Her methods look towards survival as a key factor… fashion is no longer a thing of simple beauty, but of nutrition". (Crane 2010).

Molecular Gastronomy seeks to explore the transformation of food-based materials in the kitchen, using simple cooking techniques to facilitate the creation of fictional materials.

INGREDIENTS

1 tbsp of Potato Starch
1 tsp of Glycerine
1 tsp of Vinegar
4 tbsp of Water

The ratio is 1:0.5:0.5:4 and can be multiplied for more material.

EQUIPMENT

1 Tablespoon
1 Teaspoon
Cotton Icing Bag
Piping Nozzle
Non-Stick Pan
Spatula

HEALTH & SAFETY

Take care when working with heat, materials will be extremely hot.

OTHER INFORMATION

See technical data section for more information.

See suppliers section for where to purchase materials.

Visit Miriam's website for more recipes and information.

HOW TO GUIDE

1. Measure your ingredients and mix.
2. Cook over low heat until it becomes a uniform and transparent paste. Stir continuously whilst cooking to ensure an even consistency.
3. Allow the material to cool down until warm. When warm, the material can be manipulated to create unusual surfaces, structures and forms.
4. Fill the icing bag with the warm material.
5. You can now use the icing bag to create unusual textures and surfaces or create 3D structures and forms.
6. Let it cool and dry.

USEFUL TIPS

7. If you wish to colour your material, you can add food colouring to the water ratio.
8. Any piping nozzle shape or size can be used.
9. The consistency of the material allows you to build bridges between materials or drawing 'in air'.
10. Layer structures as if you were 3D printing a shape. For better results let parts dry before continuing to build up more material.

Credits: Photography by Lydia Whitmore

Molecular Gastronomy: Material Activism by Miriam Ribul

INGREDIENTS

50g of Mushrooms

Glue
½ cup of Plain Flour
¾ cup of Water
⅙ cup of Sugar
½ tsp of Vinegar

EQUIPMENT

Hand Blender
Mixing Bowl
Cling Film
Paint Brush
Spatula
Saucepan

HEALTH & SAFETY

Be careful when working
with heat.

OTHER INFORMATION

See technical data section
for more information.

See suppliers section
for where to purchase
materials.

Visit Tamsyn 's website
for more recipes and
information.

HOW TO GUIDE

MAKING THE GLUE

1. Turn the hob onto a medium heat.
2. Add the following ingredients flour, water, sugar and vinegar to the saucepan and mix.
3. Continuously stir the mixture until it starts to thicken.
4. When the glue is a thick paste, remove from the heat and allow for it to cool.
5. Refrigerate until needed.

MUSHROOM POLYMER

6. Tear and break up 50g of mushrooms into a mixing bowl.
7. Using a hand blender, grind the mushroom pieces until they reach a pulp consistency.
8. Scoop the pulp out of the bowl and smooth out to the desired thickness onto the cling film to dry.
9. Allow the surface of the sample to dry for 24 hours or longer if required.
10. Using a paintbrush, delicately apply a thin layer of the glue and wait till dry.
11. Once the sample is fully dry, remove from the cling film and apply a thin layer of glue to the reverse side.
12. Leave to dry for 24 hour or longer if required until the sample is dry and hard.

Molecular Gastronomy: Mushroom Polymers by Tamsyn Ainsworth

INGREDIENTS

2 or 3 Fish Skins
1 glass of Water
2½ glass of Flour
1 Small Packet of Gelatine
1 Glass of Salt

EQUIPMENT

Silicone Gloves
Tray
Flat Brush
Small Brush
Scissors
Glass Bowl
Rolling Pin
Knife
Spoon

HEALTH & SAFETY

Be careful when using a knife.

OTHER INFORMATION

See technical data section for more information.

See suppliers section for where to purchase materials.

Visit Andere's website for more recipes and information.

HOW TO GUIDE

PREPARING THE FISH CUTS

1. Purchase 2 to 3 fresh fish and remove the skin from the meat.
2. Place the skin onto a tray and cover the skin with salt on both sides to remove excess oil. Leave it to dry for 24 hours, keeping the skin as flat as possible.
3. After 24 hours brush the salt away on both sides until you have the skin as clean as possible.
4. Cut the skin into micro, medium and large pieces to have a variation of sizes. Try to make geometric cuts imitating stone granite.

PREPARING THE CERAMIC BASE

5. Add the salt, flour and water to a bowl. Mix all the ingredients together with a spoon until you get a uniform paste.
6. Remove from the bowl and knead the dough until it feels as malleable as modelling clay (add more water if dough is too sticky).
7. Roll out the dough and sprinkle the fish skin pieces you have cut earlier, then knead them together to mix well.
8. Roll out the dough and cut any shape you would like (you could use a cookie cutter or stencil to help cut out shapes).
9. Coat the surface with warm liquid gelatine (to make gelatine look at the instructions of the gelatine you buy).
10. Leave the shapes to dry for 48 hours or longer if required until they look like granite ceramic tiles.

Credits: Photography by Berta Bernad

Molecular Gastronomy: Fish Granite by Andere Monjo

THE
LABORATORY

Material Alchemy

As scientific developments are shaping our future environments, a new breed of designers emerge called 'BioHackers'. BioHackers aid access to scientific materials, advocating an open source philosophy where tools and resources within the scientific realm are made available to non-scientists, to cultivate an interdisciplinary platform between researchers, scientists and designers.

Organisations such as DIYbio, HackSpace and iGem have emerged, promoting open source methodologies, as they firmly believe that innovation is cultivated when knowledge is shared. Designers such as Amy Congdon and Suzanne Lee seek to

explore the parameters of design, utilising science as a tool to create materials that are manufactured in a laboratory environment. Congdon's work aims to provoke debate and discussion around the potential ethical implications of using living materials to create bespoke products.

The Laboratory provides a platform for scientific exploration, through creative experimentation with science-based materials and processes, providing a unique DIY approach to design in the kitchen laboratory.

INGREDIENTS

300g of Boric Acid Powder
20cl of Silicone Oil
Optional Coloured Mineral Pigment

EQUIPMENT

Measuring Cups
Heat Proof Glass Bowl
Mixing Bowl
Silicone Container
Spatula

HEALTH & SAFETY

Boric acid (H_3BO_3) is a weak acid. Do not inhale or allow its vapours to reach your eyes when heated.

OTHER INFORMATION

See technical data section for more information.

See suppliers section for where to purchase materials.

Visit Laurence's website for more recipes and information.

HOW TO GUIDE

1. The preparation for boric acid caramel is similar to sugar caramel.
2. Heat the oven to 250°C.
3. Measure and mix the ingredients together and pour into a heat proof glass bowl.
4. Cook the mixture in the oven for between 1 - 3 hours until the boric acid has dissolved and the liquid is viscous and transparent. If it hasn't dissolved and turned transparent leave in the oven for longer.
5. Cool for 30-90 minutes by slowly turning the oven temperature down, to avoid thermic shock (when hot material hits cold air, it often cracks).
6. While cooling, the mass becomes solid. Before it fully cools and hardens, transfer the mixture to a silicone container.
7. To give colour to the glass, add a mineral pigment (mineral pigments are resistant to 250°C and will not burn or turn colour at that temperature). Though paprika powder is a great dye, it carbonises at 250°C.

USEFUL TIPS

8. If you find that you are left with a lot of silicone oil, utilise less in your next mix.
9. If your mixture isn't dissolving, check the temperature of your oven, maybe it isn't hot enough.
10. If your mixture isn't dissolving, make sure your glass dish is quite wide to allow for even heat distribution.

The Laboratory: Boric Acid Caramel by Laurence Humier

INGREDIENTS

1 x Egg
0.5g of Saffron Strands

EQUIPMENT

Spatula/ Palette Knife
200ml Glass Container
Measuring Cups
Scales
Pestle & Mortar
20 x 20cm Glass Slab

HEALTH & SAFETY

Take care when working with acrylic mediums, it may be toxic if inhaled or swallowed.

OTHER INFORMATION

See technical data section for more information.

See suppliers section for where to purchase materials.

Visit Laura's website for more recipes and information.

HOW TO GUIDE

SAFFRON EGG TEMPERA

1. Measure your ingredients.
2. Separate the egg yolk from the 'glaire' (egg white) and keep the 'glaire' in a container.
3. Add the saffron strands to the glaire and soak overnight.
4. The colour intensifies from pale yellow to a dark yellowish-orange.
5. Stir the mix of saffron and egg 'glaire'.
6. Once mixed it is ready to be used.

SAFFRON PIGMENT

7. Repeat steps 1 - 4.
8. Pour the mixture onto the glass slab surface.
9. Use a spatula or palette knife to spread onto the surface equally, then leave overnight to dry.
10. Once it has dried completely, scrape the dried mixture into the pestle and mortar.
11. Grind the pigment down until you get very fine particles of saffron powder.
12. Once ground, store the pigment in a dry container. This pigment can be used anytime.
13. To obtain a good quantity of saffron pigment you will need to repeat the process at least 3 times.
14. You can then mix the saffron pigment with acrylic medium to create a paint.

The Laboratory: Colour Provenance by Laura Daza

INGREDIENTS

200g of Sodium Acetate
Trihydrate
50ml of Water

EQUIPMENT

Sauce Pan
Scales
Fridge
Glass Container
Spatula
Funnel
Coffee Filter

HEALTH & SAFETY

Slightly hazardous in case of
skin contact or eye contact,
may cause irritation.
Do not ingest.

OTHER INFORMATION

See technical data section
for more information.

See suppliers section
for where to purchase
materials.

Visit Studio Aikieu's website
for more workshop and
information.

HOW TO GUIDE

1. Measure out your ingredients and pour into a pan.
2. Heat the mixture on a medium heat.
3. Stir continuously until the sodium has dissolved into a liquid.
4. Pour the mixture through the coffee filter and funnel into a clean glass, leave any solids behind in the filter.
5. Place the glass in the fridge.
6. Leave the mixture in the fridge for 15-30 minutes to cool down, until room temperature or cooler.
7. To trigger the thermic reaction, drop a small bit of sodium acetate into the mixture.
8. You can then pour the mixture onto a surface to begin sculpting with it.

USEFUL TIPS

9. If the mixture begins crystallising in the fridge, reheat the mixture and add a couple more drops of water.
10. If you find a thin transparent skin forming on the surface of your liquid whilst in the fridge, add a couple of drops of water to remove the skin.
11. Ideally what you would like to end up with is a clear liquid, but you may find you have to try this several times before you get it right.
12. Sometimes, if the solution is highly concentrated, any slight movement may trigger the solution to set off. If this happens, add a couple more drops of water.
13. You won't always get this right the first time, persevere through trial and error.

The Laboratory: Thermic Sculptures by Studio Aikieu

HIGH - TECH

Material Alchemy

High-Tech seeks to provide knowledge within the area of interactive and responsive design. High-Tech will explore smart materials such as memory shape alloys and sensors through the use of physical computing in the form of programming.

We see a growing trend emerging where designers are embracing a DIY approach to design, with vast knowledge being shared on open source platforms and technology becoming much more accessible. Learning becomes intuitive and hands on. Designers such as

Elaine Ng whose creative background has evolved from woven textiles to embracing technology, now combines the two fields together to create interactive installations, demonstrating the evolution of hybrid design practices.

High-Tech provides a platform for interactive engagement, demonstrating how cross-disciplinary platforms are emerging to create intuitive, responsive design outcomes.

INGREDIENTS

1 x Arduino Uno with USB
Cable
Bunch of Wires
1 x AA Battery Power Pack
4 x 3V AA Batteries
1 x Transistor
2 x 1.2 K Resistor
1 x Infrared Sensor
1 x 15 cm Shape Memory
Alloy (SMA)

EQUIPMENT

Wire Cutter
Stanley Knife
Electrical Tape
Scissors
Soldering Iron & Solder
1 x Computer

HEALTH & SAFETY

Please take care when using
the soldering iron as it can
become extremely hot.
SMA will get hot.

OTHER INFORMATION

See technical data section
for more information.

See Technical Section for
circuit diagram.

Visit the Fabrick Labs's

website to purchase the kit
and for more workshops
and information.
CAN YOU HACK IT?

This workshop is for more
adventurous individuals
who are up for a challenge.
We have tried to simplify
the workshop to make it
relatively easy to follow.
However, with coding and
electronics, things are
never as straightforward as
they seem, so please bear
this in mind. It is important
to consider working with
someone who has coding
and electronics knowledge
to help you problem solve
along the way. However,
don't forget that there
are many open source
platforms with helpful
forums should you need
support.

High Tech: Tectonic Circuit by The Fabrick Lab

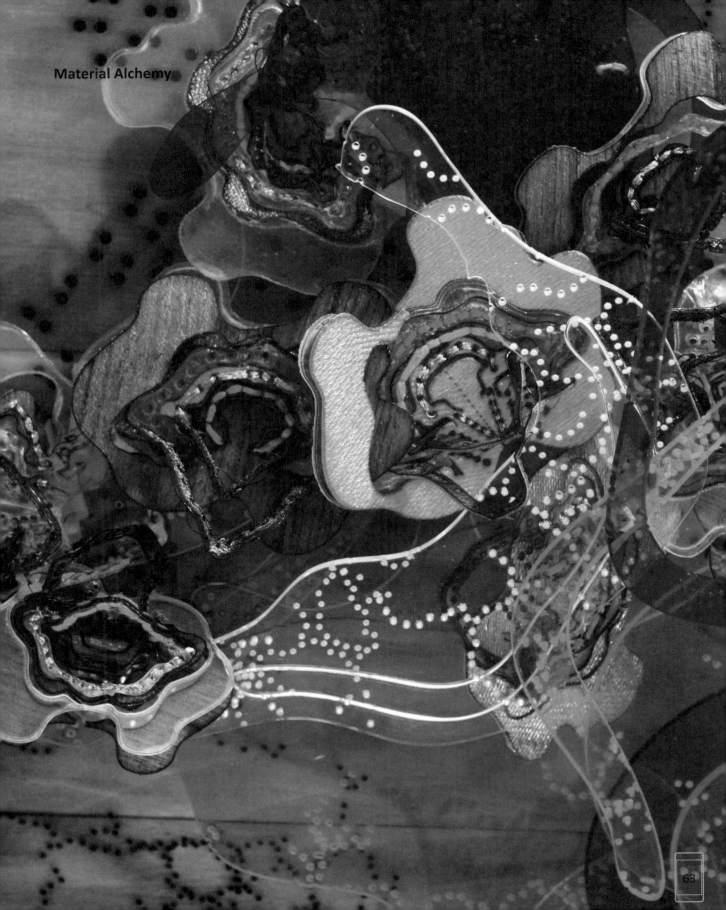

HOW TO GUIDE

BUILDING THE CIRCUIT: SWITCH PIN

1. See technical data section for Arduino diagram to help you build the circuit.
2. Solder a wire to Switch Pin A leg.
3. Solder a wire to Switch Pin K leg.
4. Solder a wire to Switch Pin E leg.
5. Solder a wire to Switch Pin C leg.
6. Connect the Switch Pin A wire to Arduino Pin 3.3v.
7. Connect the Switch Pin K wire to Arduino Pin GND.
8. Connect the Switch Pin E wire to Arduino Pin GND.
9. Connect the Switch Pin C wire to Arduino Pin 7.
10. You may wish to use colour wire to make it easier for you to follow but this isn't mandatory.

BUILDING THE CIRCUIT: SMA

11. Solder the resistor to Transistor Base leg.
12. Solder a wire to Transistor Emitter leg.
13. Wrap the SMA wire around the end of the wire on the Transistor Emitter leg. Secure with electrical tape.
14. Solder wire to Transistor Collector leg.
15. Solder a wire to the resistor on Transistor Base leg.
16. Solder the black wire from battery pack also to the Transistor Collector leg.
17. Wrap the other end of the SMA wire to the red wire from the battery pack.
18. Connect Transistor Base leg to Arduino Pin 9.
19. Connect the Transistor Collector leg to Arduino Pin 5v.
20. Plug the Arduino to the computer.

UPLOADING THE CODE

21. Download and install the Arduino software from http://arduino.cc/en/Main/Software.
22. Download the code from the Fabrick Lab website http://www.thefabricklab.com/#cg9o, click on the link 'Please click here for the code' and enter the password: fabricktectonic
23. Open up the Arduino software, this will automatically open up a new sketch.
24. Copy and paste the code (downloaded from Fabrick Lab) into the Arduino sketch.
25. Click on the tick icon to verify the

code, this will check the code for any potential errors.

26. Click on the right arrow to upload the code onto the board.

27. Insert the batteries into the battery holder.

28. Watch the SMA Wire move! The SMA wire will move gently according to the code.

TIPS

29. Make sure you have selected the correct board > Go to Tools (on the top bar), scroll down to Board and select the correct board, Arduino Uno.

30. Make sure you have selected the correct Port > Go to Tools, scroll down to Serial Port and select either /dev/tty.usbmodem... or /dev/cu.usbmodem... (usually ends in a 4 digit number such as 1411).

31. If the SMA isn't moving you might need to double check your circuit that all corresponding pieces are in their correct places.

32. It might also be worth using electrical tape and taping the connecting areas to prevent them from touching one another.

33. Please note that the image shown in relation to this workshop illustrates how Fabrick Lab have embedded SMA into a material.

Now that you have understood the basic principles of SMA, why not explore how to embed SMA into a surface to create a visual, tactile, responsive surface?

INGREDIENTS

1 x 50ml pot of Bare
Conductive Ink
5ml of Water
1 x Arduino Uno
1 x small Breadboard
14 x Jumper Wires
4 x Jumper Wires with
crocodile clip ends
4 x 1MΩ Resistors
2 x LEDs
1 x Loudspeaker
A5 sheets of paper
1 x 40mm bulldog clip
4-core cable
2 x 10mm x 40mm x 3mm
Acrylic
1 x 10mm x 40mm x
1.5mm single sided PCB
Copperboard

EQUIPMENT

Screen-printing equipment
(with 90t screen)
Computer
Soldering iron
Drill
Glue

HEALTH & SAFETY

Please take care when using
the soldering iron as it can
become extremely hot.

Do not consume the
conductive ink. If you
have an allergic reaction
to the ink, please wash off
immediately and do not
use.

OTHER INFORMATION

See technical section for
further information about
Bare Conductive Inks
and relevant templates,
diagrams etc.
Print Template
Sensor Diagram
Interactive Paper Diagram
Bulldog Clip Diagram

See suppliers section
for where to purchase
materials.

Visit Michael's website
for more workshops and
information.

CAN YOU HACK IT?

This workshop is for more
adventurous individuals
who are up for a challenge.
We have tried to simplify
the workshop to make it
relatively easy to follow.
However, with coding and
electronics, things are
never as straightforward as
they seem, so please bear
this in mind. It is important
to consider working with
someone who has coding
and electronics knowledge
to help you problem solve
along the way. However,
don't forget that there
are many open source
platforms with helpful
forums should you need
support.

High Tech: Interactive Paper by Michael Shorter

HOW TO GUIDE

SCREEN PRINTING

1. Print the print template out (see technical data section for the template).
2. Expose a screen with the template.
3. Lay down your A5 sheet on the table.
4. Place the screen on top of the paper.
5. Mix the ink with 5ml of water.
6. Pour the mixture on the edge of the bottom of the screen.
7. Ask a friend to hold the screen down or use weights.
8. Using a squeegee pull the ink up and down the screen - once each way to give it an even coating.
9. Remove the screen - wash the screen and squeegee and leave the print to dry overnight.
10. You can skip steps 1 - 9 if you have a local silk-screen printer in your area. Provide them with the template and ink and they will do the rest.

BUILDING THE CIRCUIT

11. See technical data section for interactive paper diagram to help you build the circuit.
12. Connect wire (2) to Arduino output 2.
13. Connect wire (4) to Arduino output 4.
14. Connect wire (5) to Arduino output 5.
15. Connect wire (6) to Arduino output 6.
16. Connect wire (8) to Arduino output 8.
17. Connect wire (9) to Arduino output 9.
18. Connect wire (10) to Arduino output 10.
19. Connect wire (11) to Arduino output 11.
20. Now connect these 8 wires to the breadboard (to make it easy to follow, connect them to the corresponding number, i.e. wire 2 is in Arduino output 2, so it will go in breadboard slot 2).
21. On the bread board, place a resistor between wire 2 and 4, 5 and 6, 8 and 9, 10 and 11.
22. On the breadboard, connect a wire from each slot, slots 4, 6, 9 and 11 (wire A, B, C, D). Pins 4, 6, 9 and 11 will be your sensor outputs. Pin 4 is the distance sensor, pin 6 is sensor 3, pin 9 is sensor 2 and pin 11 is sensor 1.
23. On/Off Indicator: Connect the negative leg of the LED in GND pin and the positive leg of the LED in pin 3.3V.

High Tech: Interactive Paper by Michael Shorter

24. Frequency Indicator: Connect a wire from pin 13 to slot 13 on the breadboard and a wire from pin GND to slot 14 on the breadboard.

25. Connect the positive leg of LED to slot 13 on the breadboard and the negative leg of the LED to slot 14 on breadboard.

26. Connect the speaker red wire to pin 7 and the black wire to slot 14 on the breadboard.

27. Connect the Arduino to the computer.

28. Connect 4 jumper wires (with crocodile clips) to each of the sensor wires (wire A, B, C, D).

29. Clip the other end of the wire to the paper sensors.

CODING YOUR ARDUINO

30. Download and install the Arduino software from www.arduino.cc.

31. Download the Capacitive Sensor Library from www.mrshorter.co.uk/makingpaperinteractive.dwt.

32. Connect the Arduino to the computer and open up the program, this will automatically open up a new sketch.

33. To install the Capacitive Sensor Library follow the instructions from www.arduino.cc/en/Guide/Libraries.

34. Go to Tools (on the top bar), scroll down to Board and select the correct board, Arduino Uno.

35. Go to Tools, scroll down to Serial Port and select either /dev/tty.usbmodem… or /dev/cu.usbmodem… (usually ends in a 4 digit number such as 1411).

36. Copy the code required for this workshop from www.mrshorter.co.uk/makingpaperinteractive.dwt and paste the code into the Arduino sketch.

37. Click on the tick to verify the code, this checks the code for any potential errors.

38. Click on the right arrow to upload the code onto the board.

TESTING & CALIBRATING

39. You will need to test and calibrate the code to ensure it works effectively. This is where it all gets a bit unpredictable. Hopefully it is just the distance sensor that will need calibrating.

40. In your sketch, on the top right hand

corner you will see a magnifier glass. If you click on this, it will open up the serial monitor to show you the values coming from the distance sensor.

41. When the Arduino is connected to the computer and the code is running you can open the serial monitor on the Arduino. This will display the values coming in from the distance sensor. You ideally want the sensor reading, ranging from about 200 to 1200. It is the -100 bit of the code that may need to be altered. You may need to either subtract or add more value. The reason why we need to adjust this is due to the temperamental nature of the conductive ink, and the different sized sensors people may print.

42. This should be pretty easy to do by playing about with the total 2 value in the code.

43. In the code, you will see this text: long total2 = total1 - 100; //calibration for pad...

44. Edit the number (-100) by either adding or subtracting the value.

45. For example, the number could be changed to + 200 or - 200 etc.

46. Each time you change the value, you

need to ensure you also upload the code to the Arduino.

47. Test each change until all of the sensors are working and you can hear different sounds.

MAKING THE BULLDOG CLIP CONNECTOR

48. A special connector can be made in order to ensure a good connection to the paper for all four sensors. This connector is a hacked bull-dog clip. See technical data section for bulldog clip diagram.

49. Drill a hole in the back of the bulldog clip to allow the cable to feed in.

50. Super glue the 2 pieces of acrylic inside the bulldog clip, one to each side.

51. Score three lines down the copper board to create four separate copper squares.

52. Strip the end of the cable that was threaded through the bulldog clip to expose the copper on all four of its cables.

53. Carefully solder each one of these cables to the separate sections on the copper board. Try to solder them as close to the edge as possible, being

careful to keep a low profile solder joint. At this point it is important to make sure the correct sensor cable is connected to the section of copper board that will eventually connect with your conductive ink touch points. You will be able to figure out which sensor cables go where when you look at your wiring on the Arduino end.

54. Carefully glue the wired up copper board onto the inside of the acrylic lined bulldog clip so that the copper is facing into the bite of the bulldog.

55. Plug it all together and make some noise.

TIPS

56. Calibrating the value: If the values shown is in the minus then you will need to add more value. Until you obtain a value between 200 - 1200.

57. Calibrating the value: If the value is over 1200 you may need to subtract the value until you obtain a value between 200 - 1200.

58. Calibrating the value: If your value is between 200 - 1200 but the interactive paper isn't quite working then you need to adjust the number,

test it until it is working correctly.

59. We found that sometimes 1 sensor worked and the rest didn't or that all sensors worked except for the distance sensor. We had to change the value several times until we managed to get all to work.

60. It is important that you have several printed paper samples to test with as one paper might not work properly and the other might work very well.

61. If you can't hear any sound, check your speaker.

THE
ALCHEMISTS

Material Alchemy

What is Alchemy?

The very word alchemy conjures up arcane images of powerful sorcerers with magical abilities to craft new materials and prolong life. The origins of alchemy are steeped in antiquity and secrecy. Many ancient texts written about this practice were concealed using codes riddled with duality, lending an air of mysticism and fantasy, making it difficult to decipher and often leading to a misunderstanding of the craft (Holmyard, 1990).

Unlike modern science, alchemy is often considered as a blend of scientific enquiry, mythology, magic and religion. It is a practice of a twofold nature - exoteric and esoteric.

The exoteric concentrated on the more practical, scientific side of alchemy, utilising precise methods of transmutation, whereas esoteric 'mystical alchemy' focused on the more spiritual side of alchemy, observing astrology, spirituality and nature.

Many journals written about alchemy are permeated in secrecy, bizarre ideas and often wondrous claims and contradictory assertions (Principe, 2013). Subsequently, it is often perceived as an incongruous practice, full of make-believe and wishful thinking - the creation of mad men.

But, perhaps it is this incongruous nature that inspires today's generation to revive alchemic practices. For without imagination and make-believe, innovation and creativity cannot materialise.

Craft & Alchemy

The very origins of alchemy have been debated over the centuries. Holmyard (1990) a noted scholar, believes the practice of alchemy materialised when the standards of living changed. The practice of craft such as metallurgy, weaving and carpentry surfaced, leading to the accumulation of technical knowledge in the form of coloured alloys, artificial gems and the useful properties of minerals and plants.

Craft played an important role in the discovery of new materials and processes, through experimentation and chance, leading to the development of key technologies and techniques that helped to advance the practice of alchemy.

For example metallurgists discovered the process of cupellation, dyers mastered the method of extraction, obtaining pigments from minerals, and perfumers learnt how to distil scent from plants.

Alchemists began to contemplate how this knowledge could be applied to transmute base metals into gold, leading to the alleged discovery of the legendary Philosopher's Stone.

Evolution of Alchemy in the 21st Century

Ancient stories of Nicolas Famel, the alleged founder of the Philosopher's Stone, who uncovered the mysteries of alchemy to discover the process of transmutation, enabled the alchemist to transform the ordinary into the extraordinary.

Inspired by such ideologies, Adam Brown explores this possibility through the archaic, alchemical process 'Magnum Opus'. He transposes the alchemists attempt to synthesise gold into the present using modern science. His project seeks to examine the process of transmutation through the use of modern microbiological practice to solve this ancient mystery (Brown, 2012).

Within the 21st century, scientific developments have advanced at an exponential rate, open source platforms and DIYbio organisations have led to collaborative partnerships between scientists and designers.

These collaborative partnerships harness the inherent qualities of each field in the pursuit of alternative resources, facilitating the cultivation of new materials in laboratories, through the appropriation of natural resources, leading to the synthesis of artificial versions.

History & Alchemy

Over the years, records show that notions of alchemic practices are still ambiguous and paradoxical, often linked to magic, religion, spirituality and the occult.

It is generally recognised as a protoscience, a form of chemistry and speculative philosophy that contributed to the development of modern chemistry and medicine.

Today, historical knowledge has played a major role in shaping our

Material Alchemy

future environments. Researchers and designers are excavating long forgotten materials and methodologies to uncover archaeological finds to craft new materials.

Designers such as Laura Daza and Formafantasma seek to look to the past to design for the future. They believe in the revival of tradition and culture.

Ancient processes lie dormant, ripe for rediscovery and reinterpretation with a modern twist. Blending innovation with tradition they cultivate new expressions of creativity.

As Fogelberg (2014) argues *"The reminiscence of alchemy, for their intuitive work has little to do with conventional science and involves materials from the commonplace to the curious."*

These fabled stories stir our imaginations and provide us with rich historical notions and eccentric inventions to inspire us to explore the impossible, question the improbable and venture on an expedition to uncover new discoveries.

For without magic, mythology and tradition, innovation and creativity is lost.

MATERIAL
NARRATIVES

Material Alchemy

"We are continuously seeking more from our products, wanting them to express more personality, amusement or engagement. We are after things that appeal to more of our senses." (Sansom, 2012)

In a digital age, we are becoming more connected with our technological devices, using technology as a form of communication and documentation, capturing our memories and recording special moments in time.

Although technological advances have contributed positively to society's growth and development, we have seen an overwhelming reliance and sense of disconnection with society and the self.

This has led to the development of products and ideas that facilitate the process of reconnection to regain a sense of normality in a hyper data driven world.

No Noise is a concept devised by Selfridges to re-evaluate the retail experience where shopping becomes a journey of discovery, an opportunity for escapism and meditation. Products become debranded to shift the focus back to value, experience and poignant narratives.

Consumers are no longer buying products based purely on aesthetic value, instead, they require a more intrinsic value that enables them to connect on a deeper level. This has led to narrative enquiry, utilising storytelling as a tool in the transfer or sharing of knowledge to allow us to build tangible, emotional connections.

Material Narratives showcase the works of designers who approach materials in a whimsical and imaginative way, whether as a tool to transform ancient rituals and traditions, to convey narrative and make-believe, or to facilitate a sense of connectedness between object and user.

MORPHOLOGIES

The Alchemists: Sarah Linda Forrer

Material Alchemy

The ancient Egyptians regarded beauty as a sign of holiness. They were pioneers of embellishment. For both men and women, beauty and body care were an integral part of their everyday lives.

Fascinated by the idea that cosmetics are not only used for aesthetics but also have a magical and ritual purpose, a collection of facial skin care tools inspired by ancient Egyptian beliefs and habits were fashioned.

These objects combine excavated findings with artefact materials to become new minerals and soft fossils. Haptic textures and morphing shapes form the tools to create mixtures and masks, to apply to the face and to clean the skin.

Trophies of imagination, Morphologies connects beauty and spirituality by bringing another dimension into our everyday skin care rituals.

Credits: Photographer: Matthijs Mentink, Models: Stella, Kim & Victor

POOR TOOLS

The Alchemist: Studio Fludd

Material Alchemy

Poor Tools evolved from a project set by design collective How We Dwell.

Given only a basic set of unusual tools and materials, and left isolated on the beautiful, deserted La Certosa Island in Venice. Studio Fludd allowed their imaginations to run wild, deciding to live and interpret the island as a spread residence, using the landscape and make-believe to craft an imaginary dwelling.

This process resulted in an intriguing dialogue between materiality and man.

Through scavenging and hunting, they located natural and artificial objects, which they crafted into a series of artefacts that conveyed the narrative of the wild and chaotic landscape of La Certosa.

The project highlights the value of make-believe, how creativity and imagination can enable us to become resourceful as a means to survive, and the importance of re-using discarded materials to create a more sustainable environment.

WONDER MATERIALS

www.clemenswinkler.com

New material technologies work hard to come up with materials that don't exist in nature by transforming the immanent properties of physical matter, energy and geometries into new visible and audible phenomena.

Today we see new material technologies colliding with the imaginative worlds of human wishes. This could see the reinvention of universal topics concerning experience and desire, how to mutate, how to disappear and reappear or how to get energised.

The Laboratory of Wondermaterials investigates the potential of plausible materiality that unbound risks, benefits or desires to re-imagine new relationships with our environment.

Today, new materials are considered to be smart and durable, but what are their realms and how do we perceive them? Where is their potential embedded to drive us into new sensations and bodily experiences, to stimulate our imagination, to let us embody with our environment in an unprecedented way?

In the past, alchemy allowed us to synthesise new elements based on our

The Alchemist: Clemens Winkler

Material Alchemy

experiences and imagination. Accordingly, every synthesised element was bounded to a narrative, which affords a reliance on creativity.

Retrospectively, that way of discovering could be reasonable for modern Material Sciences within Physics, Chemistry, Biology, to build on phenomena and personal stories besides causality – from the lab into the kitchen.

Wondermaterials proposes a practical and critical approach to the genuine advances of new physical resonances between a human need for narrative and upcoming technologies. So what does the new playground for Wondermaterials look like? Showing different phenomena from material energies through computational methods, open up different wonders by preserving the event of fascination.

This laboratory will reflect on our relationship to new technologies and materials in science and in culture, considering materials as carriers of what Bachelard calls the *"unlimited capacities of imagination"* (Bachelard, 1983)

VÆTTIR

www.aikieu.com

Vættir is a poetic project that is comprised of a collection of products that have been designed specifically for plants, highlighting their personalities and needs.

Inspired by the Swiss Declaration of Plant Rights, which affords plants rights as living entities, the project is intended to be a playful look at the curious nature of our relationship with flora and fauna.

Each piece in the collection is designed with a specific plant, or type of plant, in mind, looking at creating the perfect vessel and tools that reflect their characteristics.

The resulting pieces are a hand crafted collection that seeks to engage people with plants in more meaningful ways. In researching this project numerous stories were collected from people who have had special relationships with a plant in their lives.

The overwhelming trend that ran through all of the tales is both the plant's personality, and perhaps most importantly, the therapeutic effect of caring for them in a society where it is all too easy to be disconnected from nature.

Credits: In collaboration with Amy Congdon, Photographer: JJ Hastings, Makers: Aimee Bollu & Melody Vaughan

The Alchemist: Studio Aikieu

Material Alchemy

MATERIAL
INTERACTIONS

Material Alchemy

Technological advances have led to new methods of production and manufacture: the birth of addictive manufacture (3D printing), has revolutionised the manufacturing industry.

It is predicted that in the future consumers will own a 3D printer in their own home, enabling them to be in control of their own manufacture of goods. In response to this we see an increasing desire for individuality. The emerging trend 'anti-mass manufacture' illustrates designers and consumers revolting against homogeneous design.

Low-tech, small-scale factories are being created to facilitate the production of one-off bespoke craft, where each design is never the same.

The production of goods is focused more on the process of making, how a material may react or change, and the interactions between man and material. These low-tech handcontrolled machines encourage consumers to be more involved with the production process, facilitating a stronger reconnection between the maker and the end user, providing a sense of honesty and transparency in an area that is normally hidden.

We see the material itself becoming the subject, the process and the outcome. Relationships begin to evolve between man, machine, and material; the three become inextricably linked.

Material Interactions focus on the process of making, how new technological developments give rise to new methods of production that can re-establish a more meaningful connection between man and materiality.

From the celebration of low-tech materials, materials that facilitate interaction, or revive lost rituals and traditions to materiality and the brain, each designer featured in this section takes an avant-garde approach to the exploration of new material connections.

THE PEDDLER

The Alchemist: Unfold

Material Alchemy

The Peddler introduces a new brand of craft oriented perfumery that is committed to the know-how and the beauty of the *'materia prima'*. Absolutely organic and related to the magic of the celebration of the senses, here perfume and olfactory installations show a new way of experiencing scent.

Working on different domains where perfumery can be applied, Barnabé Fillion explores the limits of the territory, the different processes of creating and new directions to underpin his perfumes.

For Maison et Objet, he collaborated with different artists and designers to create a magical world of scents, where both innovation and tradition play an important role, linking together nature, art and technology.

Together with Barnabé Fillion and Perla Valtierra, Unfold created a set of objects that resemble alchemical tools and utensils to revisit the process of transformation in alchemy.

The three diffusers and receptacles, were produced using Unfold's unique ceramic 3D printing device. The 3D printing machine invites visitors to interact and be intimately involved in the process, placing real emphasis on the ritual and experience of perfume.

Credits: Project by Barnabé Fillion, Collaborators: Sebastien Preschoux and Perla Valtierra

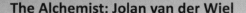

GRAVITY STOOL

www.jolanvanderwiel.com

The Gravity Stool's distinct shape is fashioned by magnetic fields and the powers of gravity.

Departing from the idea that everything is influenced by gravity, the project intended to manipulate this natural phenomenon by exploiting its power: magnetism.

The positioning of the magnetic fields in the machine, opposing each other, has largely determined the final shape of the Gravity Stool. The forms and products are characterised by the freakish and organic shapes that are so typical of nature itself.

The potential in how we combine technology with natural phenomena to craft new tools is integral in allowing new forms to take shape.

Credits: Photographer: Jac van der Wiel

The Alchemist: Jolan van der Wiel

THE ARCHEO MILL

www.arabeschidilatte.org

In the future there will be an intimate physical reconnection between the things we consume, the artisans who create them and the material itself.

Consumers will be involved in the manufacture of their own food, experiencing first hand the manufacturing process from production to consumption. Knowledge lost will be revived, bringing fascination and ancient stories behind the food we consume.

The Archeo Mill is an interactive installation where visitors are given the opportunity to experience the 'archaeology of taste'. Grinding and kneading, making the flour with their own hands, visitors go back to basics to establish an intimate relationship with materials and the process of making.

The Alchemists: Arabeschi di Latte

Material Alchemy

An 'archaeological harvesting' for a sort of primordial baking is staged, where pure and preserved ingredients of the past are seen as protagonists of the future for their properties, endurance and spontaneous availability.

Once the flour is created, the visitors are invited to use the ingredients to prepare tasty fresh food to eat and share. Reminding us what will always make human sociality so extraordinary is the deeply rooted concept of sharing food.

Baking the past to make the future.

Credits: Photographer: Amandine Alessandra & Food Styling: Francesca Sarti

93

The human mind is a thought factory, producing around 70,000 thoughts per day. Due to the complexity of the brain and the importance of our unconscious mind for the creative process we are currently unable to tap the full potential of the human mind. Imagine a device that could physically harness the boundless energy and the instantaneous nature of a thought to aid and innovate the process of creation. The Thought Harvester is an invertebrate, artificial organism based on recent research into cerebral organoids. These lab-grown mini-brains develop in a spinning bioreactor and feature defined regions such as cerebral cortex and meninges.

THE THOUGHT HARVESTER

The central nervous system of this semi-living extends to the tentacles, which are touch-sensitive, muscular structures that enable interconnection with a human system. With these, the device can send and receive impulses enabling it to form a symbiosis with its human. Its DNA is engineered to grow a strong yet lightweight bone structure, protecting the inner organs, while ensuring compatibility with the user. The skin is equipped with sensory cells that detect light, scents and physical contact. Its pores serve a respiratory function and nutrients are ingested through the skin. The nervous system is electrochemical and thus able to communicate with an external entity through electrical impulses. With its implanted neural interface, the Harvester can tap into an external network accessing the latest research and general information relevant for the user. Once synchronisation is achieved between the device and the human brain, the Thought Harvester can tap into the neural network of humans. It will help the mind to focus, and allow its user to explore material properties such as shape, colour, weight and other visual and haptic information. It then harvests thoughts and imagination that originate during this process. This virtual yet physical approach could lead to a more organic and intuitive process of making.

Credits: Photographer: Robert Klebenow, Hair & Make up: Claudia Rotoli, Model: Sophie Yall (IMG), Embroiderer: Amy Congdon & 3D Modelling: Anne-May Abel

The Alchemists: Ann-Kristin Abel

Material Alchemy

MATERIAL
PROVENANCE

Material Alchemy

Anthropocene: the Age of Man — a geological term used to describe the impact of man on the earth's ecosystem. How do we counteract this to protect our environment whilst still maintaining our way of living? Conscious design and eco-living are at the forefront of our minds. Depleting resources, rise in temperature and sea levels, and polar ice caps melting, all highlight the importance of embracing positive change by going back to basics.

Designers are re-evaluating their approach to material consumption by exploring locality and sustainable resources. Unassuming humble materials become the focus of beauty, celebrating the mundane and overlooked. Hyun Jin Jeong's eloquently titled project Earth Dyeing is a poignant response to the potential ramifications of material consumption on our future environment, urging designers and consumers to look closer to home in the search of more sustainable methods of production. Agricultural and industrial waste form the basis of 21st century design exploration, in the creation of new materials for design application by cultivating waste in the form of a closed loop cycle.

We see a resurgence of ancient processes and traditions seeking to learn from our ancestors by scouring archives, visiting tribes and remote villages to learn the ancient history of long forgotten materials. Time-honoured crafts, which have been rendered worthless, are being re-examined and revived by designers (Libbysellers, 2014).

Material Provenance seeks to showcase the works of designers whose research explores key ideals such as preservation, design ecology and revival, in the hope to design for a more sustainable future.

DE NATURA FOSSILIUM

When Mount Etna erupted on 20th November 2013, the dramatic event was broadcast by a haunting noise of rumbling stones and a vast plume of dark smoke that completely obscured the sun. After the smoke, black earthen debris began showering down over the villages and cities within the immediate vicinity of the mountain.

"Mount Etna is a mine without miners – it is excavating itself to expose its raw materials." (Formafantasma, 2014)

Studio Formafantasma, in collaboration with Gallery Libby Sellers, present De Natura Fossilium an investigation into the cultures surrounding this particularly Sicilian experience to bring both the landscape and the forces of nature together as facilities for production.

As in their previous projects Autarchy (2010) and Moulding Tradition (2009), Formafantasma question the link between tradition and local culture and the relationship between objects and the idea of cultural heritage, refusing to accept locality as touristic entertainment. Instead, the work is a different expedition in which the landscape is not passively contemplated but restlessly sampled, melted, blown, woven, cast and milled. From the more familiar use of basalt stone to their extreme experiments with lava in the production of glass and the use of lavic fibres for textile, Formafantasma's explorations and resulting objects realise the full potential of the lava as a material for design.

In homage to Ettore Sottsass, the great maestro of Italian design and an avid frequenter of the volcanic Aeolian islands, this new body of work takes on a linear, even brutalist form. Geometric volumes have been carved from basalt and combined with fissure-like structural brass elements to produce stools, coffee tables and a clock. The clock itself is deconstructed into three basalt horizontal plates to represent the passing of hours, minutes and seconds. A brass movement spins around the plates,

The Alchemists: Formafantasma

Material Alchemy

shifting three different ages of lavic sand that have been sampled from three different sites on Stromboli.

Lavic glass, procured by remelting Etna's rocks, has been mouth-blown into unique vessels or cast into box-like structures that purposefully allude to the illegal dwellings and assorted buildings that have developed at the foot of the volcano. Drawing on their own vocabulary, these solitary glass boxes and mysterious black buildings have been finished with such archetypal Formafantasma detailing as cotton ribbons and Murano glass plaques.

By returning the rocks to their original molten state Formafantasma are reversing the natural timeline of the material and forcing a dialogue between the natural and man-made. A black, obsidian mirror that is suspended on a brass structure and balanced by lavic rocks continues this line of narrative, as the semiprecious glass like stone is produced only when molten lava is in contact with water. Formafantasma have also investigated the tensile properties of lavic fibre and woven two different wall hangings. These pieces combine illustrative references to both the Greek mythological gods of Mount Etna and the microscopic views of lavic rock's geological strata as ascertained through the designers' collaboration with the Volcanologist Centre of Catania (INGV). As a sustainable alternative to carbon fibre, Formafantasma's use of lavic fibre has effectively reappropriated a conventionally high tech material for artisanal ends.

Credits Photographer: Luisa Zanzani, Concept, Design: Andrea Trimarchi, Simone Farresin, Development: Francesco Zorzi, Nicola Lorini, Emile Kirsch, Bettina Bohm, Luisa Zanzani, Francesco Pace, Production: INGV/Catania (Rosanna Corsaro, Lucia Miraglia). Carl Aubock/Vienna, Berengo Studio, Leerdam Glass Museum, Textiel Museum Tilburg, Sergio Grasso, Teun Vinken, Giuseppe Amendolia, Special thanks: PS-Michela Pelizzari, Federica Sala. Supported by Creative Industries Fund NL, collection available through Gallery Libby Sellers, London.

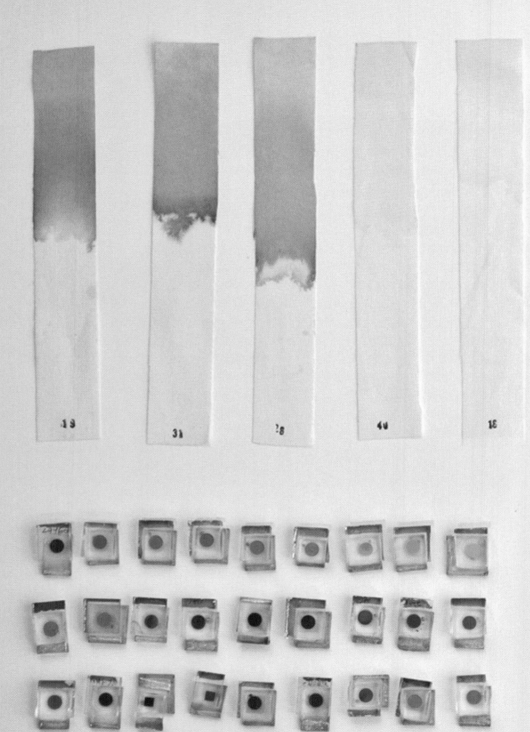

The Alchemist: Marjan van Aubel

Material Alchemy

In this collection everyday objects such as glassware absorbs energy from daylight. It gathers energy from the light around it, whether you are drinking from your glass or have left it on the side, it is constantly working to gather energy. The solar cells are completely integrated into the objects themselves, a unique self-sufficient system. When you put the glass away, the specially designed cabinet itself collects and stores this energy; it's a way to gather and harvest energy all within one room. The cabinet works as a battery. This power can be adapted in many ways, from charging your phone to powering a light source. Within each glass is a photovoltaic layer of dye synthesised solar cell. This means that the properties of colour are being used to create an electrical current. This technology was invented by Michael Graetzel at EPFL. It is a technique based on the process of photosynthesis in plants. Like the green chlorophyll which absorbs light energy, the colours in these cells collect energy. Graetzel uses a porous titanium dioxide layer soaked with photosensitive dye – a natural pigment

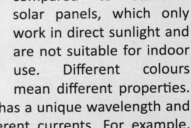

THE ENERGY COLLECTION

extracted from the juice of blueberries or spinach. He discovered that the dye that gives the red or blue colour to berries, gives off an electron when light strikes it. One side of the glass is positive, the other negative, and when the cell is exposed to light, the dye transmits its electrons to the titanium dioxide and releases an electronic current. The glassware uses sunlight as a sustainable source of energy, but can also work under diffused light. This makes them much more efficient for use inside the home compared to standard solar panels, which only work in direct sunlight and are not suitable for indoor use. Different colours mean different properties. Each colour has a unique wavelength and collects different currents. For example, blueberries and raspberries have their own voltages and levels of efficiency according to the colour spectrum.

Credits: Photographer: Wai Ming Ng, Michael Graetzel lab at Ecole Polytechnic Federale Lausanne, Solaronix Lausanne, EPFL+ECAL Lab and Imperial College London.

EARTH DYEING

www.earthdyeing.com

Earth Dyeing is a critical project that seeks to identify new materials and processes for textile applications.

The project explores overlooked materials such as soil to demonstrate the value they have as an alternative resource.

The potential of earth as a material for textile colouration is wide reaching; using soil as a dye may seem unorthodox but people have been using soil to colour their garments for centuries.

This ancient tradition is being revived in response to the consequences of synthetic textile dyeing in the 21st century.

45 different soils were collected from various geographical locations across South Korea and the UK. These samples were then transformed into a rich palette of colours, creating a range of vivid hues including ochre, rust and sienna that can be used for textile applications.

The rediscovery of everyday materials from nature and the revival of lost traditions are essential for a sustainable future (Elkin, 2011).

The Alchemist: Hyun Jin Jeong

The Alchemist: Aagje Hoekstra

COLEOPTERA

Inspired by biomimicry and the rapid advances insects make in human consumption, has led to the cultivation of meal worms, to see what positive values insects have on society and the environment.

In the Netherlands, meal worms are bred for the animal food industry. Meal worms are the larval form of the meal worm beetle, which dies three to four months after laying its eggs, because the beetle is at the end of its life cycle, it is seen as waste. Insect farms are throwing away 30 kilograms of dead beetles every week.

The beetles shield contains a polymer called chitin, which can be transformed into chitosan. Coleoptera is a project that explores this excessive waste and turns the waste into a new form of insect plastic for future material applications.

MATERIAL

APPROPRIATION

Material Alchemy

The manipulation of materials in the 21st century has advanced to unprecedented heights. Designers are increasingly becoming more fascinated in the field of biotechnology as an instrument in the creation of future synthetic materials. Portrayed as contemporary alchemy, this nascent technology seeks to harness living organisms by altering the DNA in the attempt to design new living matter (Fogelberg, 2014).

With the rise of open source platforms and DIYbio organisations popping up in every city, the future of biotechnology will evolve as we continue to share and adapt ideas and research. A future, that some believe, holds the key in the preservation of life on earth.

"The intersection of design and science allows both fields to explore new questions. Developing a closer relationship with biology allows designers to begin to imagine a future with no waste. Understanding how to program living organisms, points to a new frontier of coding—beyond software, into materiality" (Ideo, 2011).

Material appropriation is not new in the history of mankind. During the Stone Age rocks were adapted to form tools for hunting, around 6000 BC we learned how to melt and fuse metals. The diversity of materials has become copious, as we learn to adapt our natural resources to craft new materials. In the future, rather than crafting materials from the 'tree of life' we will be cultivating them from the Synthetic Kingdom Elfick and Endy (2014).

Material Appropriation showcases the works of designers who seek to explore how they attempt to shape and bend biology to their will. Their work highlights the potential benefits of cultivating home grown materials within a 'kitchen-laboratory' setting in the future, whilst trying to address the ethical ramifications of altering nature's DNA.

The underlying theme that runs parallel in each of their work, is questioning what our material future may be if we continue to experiment with emerging technologies and the life sciences.

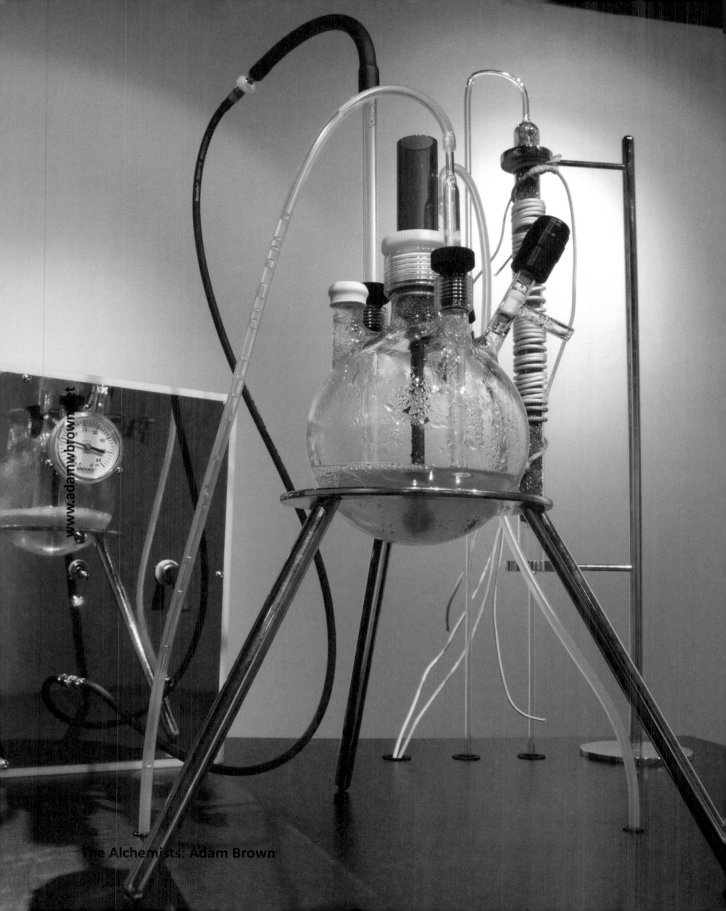

The Alchemists: Adam Brown

MICROBIAL ALCHEMY

Historically, magnum opus was an alchemical process that incorporated a personal, spiritual and chemical method for creating the Philosopher's Stone, a mysterious red coloured substance that was capable of transmuting base matter into the noble metal of gold. Discovering the principles of the Philosopher's Stone was one of the defining and at the same time seemingly unattainable objectives of western alchemy.

The Great Work of the Metal Lover (GWML) is a living biochemical installation that transposes the alchemist's historical attempt to synthesise gold into the present, and combines it with today's increasing interest in primitive but robust organisms that played a crucial role in the origin of life on Earth — extremophiles.

Extremophiles are micro organisms that are able to survive and flourish in physically and/or chemically extreme conditions that would kill most of the life on our planet. It is believed that extremophiles hold the key to understanding how life may have originated due to their unique ability to metabolise toxic substances like uranium, arsenic and gold chloride.

They are currently being studied in order to transform them into bio-filters to bioremediate industrial sites that mankind has polluted with heavy metals and other toxic substances.

Unlike the ancient alchemical process used to create the secret magnum opus substance, GWML makes use of an extremophilic bacterium that can survive hostile conditions within a reducing atmosphere of carbon dioxide, heavy metals, and hydrogen in a customised glass bioreactor.

Cupriavidus Metallidurans bacteria metabolises toxic gold chloride and produce copious amount of nano size gold particles within a biofilm matrix, which can then be harvested and transformed into 24 carat gold leaf.

While the project solves the ancient riddle through the use of modern microbiology, it also questions our human centric obsession with greed and the creation of wealth. Finally, the installation speaks directly to the scientific preoccupation with trying to shape and bend biology to our will, essentially questioning the ethical and political ramifications of attempting to breach nature.

Credits: In collaboration with Kazem Kashefi

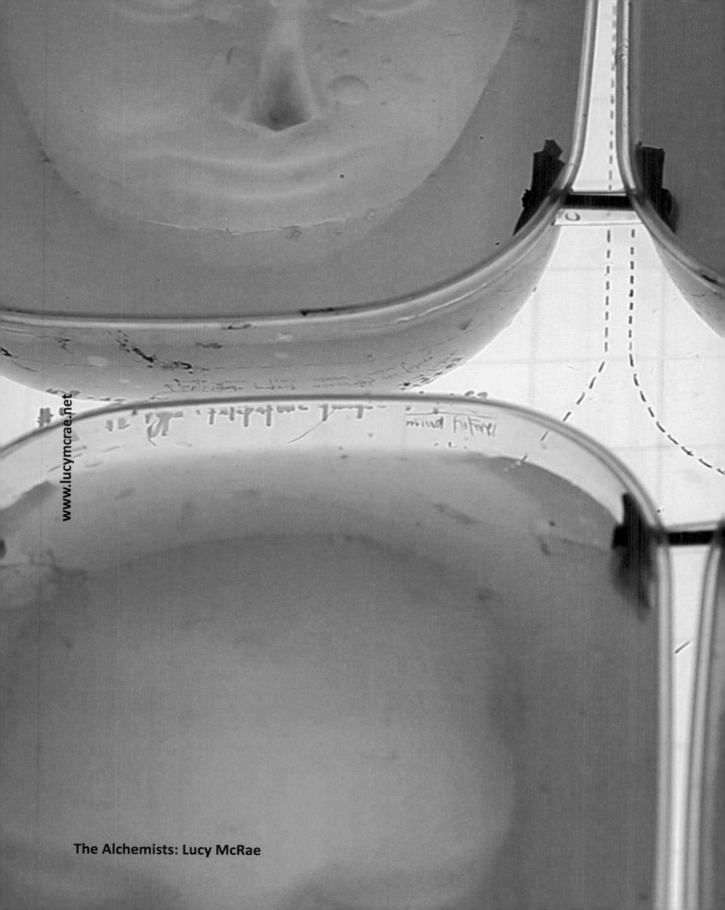

The Alchemists: Lucy McRae

MAKE YOUR MAKER

Taking on the domain of genetic manipulation and human cloning Make Your Maker written and directed by Lucy McRae responds to the idea that 'Food and the body are inseparable', delivering a world where clones are edible, their sensory effects absorbed through the body.

We see a lone woman fastidiously prepare and distil human body parts, using her own body as a test bed, fusing gender and blending ego like a chef constitutes food.

Her laboratory references the wet and somewhat grotty kitchens found in dim-sum markets, the basement housing her inventions.

We see her curiosity in process, operating an assembly line of kitchen appliances big enough to steam a body.

Duplicates are cut precisely with facial cutters, dissected according to her mathematical matrix, sealed and then packaged for consumption.

BIOPLASTIC FANTASTIC

www.johannaschmeer.com

Bioplastic Fantastic investigates new types of products and interactions which might emerge from material innovations in the fields of bio and nanotechnology. It speculates on the future design and use of domestic products made from enzyme enhanced bioplastics. The concept is based on a recent scientific breakthrough in the synthesis of functioning biological cells made from polymers and enzymes. Seven products provide all nutrients and energy needed for a human to survive. They produce water, vitamins, fibre, sugar, fat, protein and minerals through biological processes, and are powered by artificial photosynthesis.

The products are designed to be part of a biologically influenced domestic space, and their aesthetics are not machine-like or lab-like, to emphasise their domesticity and the design opportunities that might

The Alchemists: Johanna Schmeer

Material Alchemy

arise with these new types of materials: to make design more sensual, and less technical, less industrial. The loss of the natural sensuality of traditional food is substituted by a designed, artificial sensuality.

All of the product designs are based on bacteria which have similar functions in nature. They use the functional part of the biological circuit (enzymes), and combine this with non-living matter (bioplastic). As interactive products are growing closer and closer to the body, and scientists are making advances in the use of living matter in materials suitable for product design, it is feasible that soon biochemical processes will be taking place in and on our technological devices.

Credits: Photographer: Christian Schmeer, Model: Maria Lee-Warren

DeCellular

031 BACON   12013

NOTES

Precut pork bacon
5 days decell
Salted dye bath (3hrs)
Silica dried

The Alchemist: The Kitchen

DECELLULAR

Increasingly, designers are becoming interested in how processes developed within the field of biotechnology can be explored as new ways of producing materials outside of the traditional laboratory setting.

DeCellular is a materials research project that explores the technique of decellularising organs; a process that involves removing the cells from an organ, such as a kidney. Once stripped of their cells, only the extracellular matrix remains, containing materials such as collagen and elastin, which make up the architecture of the organ.

The aim in regenerative medicine research is to be able to, at some point in the future, reseed a decellularised organ with a patient's own cells and then implant the organ. However, in this project the decellularised meat is explored as a material in its own right, experimented with and pushed to its aesthetic limits.

The project highlights the unexpected results that can occur from the cross contamination of ideas and techniques between design and science. The outcome of the project was a custom-made glass bio-chamber that is used for the process of decellularisation and a range of samples that showcase this new material.

The samples were treated using various traditional textile techniques such as dyeing, tanning and printing. The resulting material archive showcases a bottom-up approach, exploring what can be done with existing biotechnology protocols and techniques when combined with textile design processes.

Through cataloguing these experiments with decellularised meat, a new materiality is developing, highlighting a potential future where our material landscape is very different to how it stands today.

The overall aim of the project is to begin to ask what our material future might be as designers and artists continue to experiment with emerging technologies and the life sciences.

Credits: Project by: Amy Congdon & JJ Hastings
Photographer: JJ Hastings

TECHNICAL
DATA

Material Alchemy

All workshops featured in this book have been tried and tested by the contributors and where possible, they have clearly outlined potential health and safety risks associated with that particular workshop.

The contributors, author and publisher strongly advise that prior to undertaking any workshops that a full risk assessment is carried out.

The purpose of a risk assessment is to identify hazards and evaluate any associated risks to health and safety arising from activities undertaken, enabling informed decisions to be made to eliminate or minimise any risk of harm to those who may be affected.

It is important to undertake a risk assessment prior to carrying out any of the activities presented in this publication.

We also strongly advise that where possible, to carry out these workshops in consultation with a professional of that particular field. The majority of these workshops are not suitable for children, and it is not advised that children participate in these workshops.

To undertake any of the workshops presented in this publication is to do so at your own risk. The author and publisher will not be held accountable for the use or misuse of the information in this book.

The technical data chapter provides additional, valuable information, technical diagrams and lab sheets to support your learning within the workshop section of the publication.

LOW-TECH

Workshop 1: Squishy Circuits

Squishy Circuits is made up of two important components that make it conductive: salt and water. Salt is a good conductor of electricity but not as conductive as metal.

Salt is made up of sodium and chlorine ions. An ion is an atom or molecule which has an electrical charge (Home Science Tools, 2014).

Salt in its dry form isn't conductive, it needs to be combined with water. When you place salt in water, the water molecules pull the ions apart so that they float freely. These ions are what carry electricity through the water. The more salt you add to the mix the more conductive it becomes.

Although you are using very low voltage batteries, it is not advisable to mix electricity with water (Thomas, 2014).

Workshop 2: Touch Sensitive

Touch Sensitive workshop utilises Bare Conductive paint. The paint provides a great platform for discovering, playing, repairing and designing with electronics.

You can use the paint for a range of applications, from creative to highly technical projects. The paint can be used as a liquid wire to draw or print graphical circuits, or even as a conductive adhesive eliminating the need for soldering equipment.

This makes it a great prototyping tool for makers of all ages. The paint also comes in handy for repairing electronics, such as PCBs, or even old TV remotes. You can use the paint to create capacitive surfaces, so you can add interactivity onto almost any object. It can also be used alongside electrical components, prototyping materials, PCBs, microcontrollers, e-textiles, and conductive thread.

Technical Data: Low-Tech

Material Alchemy

It is a nontoxic, solvent free, water soluble, air-drying paint that is child friendly, making it great for use at home or in the classroom

The paint works on many materials including paper, plastic, textiles and conventional electronics. Simply apply with a brush, roller, or screen print, leave to dry for 5 minutes, and start building interactive surfaces (Nelson, 2014).

Workshop 3: Graphite Sounds

The mineral graphite is the softest of the structural formations that develop from carbon. Graphite consists of many layered carbon sheets of only one-atom-thickness, each of them highly electrically and thermally conductive. Apart from winning a Nobel prize when being in its one-layered form (graphene), graphite is used for making steel, dry lubricants, and electrodes. But most importantly it is the main ingredient in 'lead pencils', which do not only serve as an everyday useful writing utensil, but has also supported artists to produce drawings with intricate shadings for hundreds of years. Apart from graphite, pencils contain wax or clay fillers to bond the graphite and achieve different grades.

While graphene is highly conductive, the stacked graphite can have a fairly high resistance. This might not be of advantage if you want to make electrical connections such as wires, but you can use it to produce beautiful hand-drawn sensors and resistors.

If you intend to use graphite in its powder form, ensure you wear a mask and use in a well ventilated room to prevent inhalation (Greinke, 2014).

MOLECULAR GASTRONOMY

Workshop 4: Material Activism

The ingredients from Material Activism are nontoxic and can be easily sourced, leading to an inventive 'mixing' approach with improvised ingredients for different creative outcomes.

By altering the ratio of the ingredients will transform the outcome of the material, adding glycerine and vinegar to the mix will make the material soft and flexible, replace these with oil and a lower water ratio, creates a cement-like structure.

The handling of these materials do not require specialist knowledge, the format of the workshop has been designed in the style of simple cooking processes. As a nontoxic mixture it can be used safely and disposed of where it will naturally biodegrade.

The resulting material has similar properties to plastic and silicone that is used in several design products and prototypes and can therefore act as a sustainable alternative to it. The base of the material can be categorised as a bioplastic. Bioplastics are increasingly used at an industrial scale, as a plastic substitute derived from sustainable and renewable resources (Ribul, 2014).

Workshop 5: Mushroom Polymer

Mushrooms are fungi fruits. As recycling agents, they are able to decompose dead organic matter into new compost, controlling nitrogen levels in the soil and therefore aiding new natural growth.

Mushrooms can cultivate from a variety of waste by-products and substrates. To reproduce, spores are released, which then mate with other spores or tendrils and grow to form new fruits.

Mushroom Polymer creates a sustainable purpose for mushroom fungus, in response to environmental and social issues of waste and pollution.

Technical Data: Molecular Gastronomy

Material Alchemy

Mushrooms have a soft, absorbent, fibrous texture that can be easily broken down to form pulps and pastes. Methods used mirror the natural processes taken by mushrooms when decomposing: fragmentation, penetration, mixing and reduction. Natural forces become the design process for an alliance with nature (Ainsworth, 2014).

Workshop 6: Fish Granite

The Fish Granite is a composite material with an appearance of a stone-like surface commonly used in architecture and interiors The term 'granite' comes from grain, and makes reference to a congregation of minerals and rocks with similar textures and slight variations on composition and origin.

Typical granites normally consist of fragments of quartz, feldspar crystals or mica and can be predominantly white, pink, or grey in colour, depending on their mineralogy.

The purpose of this material is obviously not to be used as a construction stone, but to develop a granite recipe using only edible ingredients to mimic the surface qualities of granite.

Curing fish skin and then mixing salt, flour and water together to create the stone base and using a gelatine binder to finish off the surface, you can produce a hard stone-like composition uniformly textured very similar to natural granites (Monjo, 2014).

THE
LABORATORY

Workshop 7: Boric Acid Caramel

Boric acid is mainly composed of minerals, and is a component of Pyrex glass. This acid is soluble in cold water and melts at 480°F. It is sold in drug stores.

Boric acid (H_3BO_3) is a weak acid, used for medical applications (antiseptic and antibacterial) and also as a neutron absorber in the nuclear industry. Do not inhale or allow its vapours to reach your eyes when heated.

Sugar caramel is similar to glass. Simply prepare a compound of sugar and water, then heat. During heating, caramelising reactions occur. Depending on the particular temperature and duration of heating and cooling, the cooled caramel will be more or less coloured, and more or less viscous, and might vitrify (transform into glass).

The resulting material is a solid with the structural disorder of a liquid, and has an amorphous structure (rather than crystalline). During the cooling of the caramel solution, crystallisation does not have time to occur, so the solution becomes a glass.

While sugar caramel results from a series of chemical reactions, boric acid caramel develops from a physical transformation, a fusion. Both materials look alike on a macroscopic level. They are both brittle and water soluble (Humier, 2013).

Extract from the ebook
Cooking Material. Could molecular gastronomy help discover new matter? by Laurence Humier with the collaboration of Audrey Tardieu.

Under the patronage of Triennale Design Museum and the Fédération Wallonie-Bruxelles support.

Technical Data: The Laboratory

Material Alchemy

Workshop 8: Colour Provenance

Colour Provenance is a visual investigation and interpretation into the ancient world of colour. In-depth research was undertaken to revive ancient rituals and alchemy techniques to manufacture natural pigments of colour.

In the 16th century, egg tempera was used as a traditional water-soluble painting medium. It provides a satin finish to the surface it is applied to.

Saffron is a plant source, its botanical name is Crocus Sativus, when used to create pigment it gives a warm orange to bright yellow colour (Daza, 2014).

Workshop 9: Thermic Sculptures

Sodium Acetate Trihydrate is the sodium salt of acetic acid. It is commonly used in a supersaturated solution to produce heat and crystals.

Cooling sodium acetate below its melting point will cause a chemical reaction, the liquid solidifies and crystallises. Sodium acetate is often found in hand warmers due to its exothermic reaction, which gives off heat and can be reused multiple times.

You can purchase sodium acetate in its raw form, pure sodium acetate and sodium trihydrate, both of these do the same thing.

HIGH TECH

Workshop 10: SMA

One of the Shape Memory materials that have been explored by many architects and textile designers is Shape Memory Alloy (SMA).

Shape Memory Alloy is considered as a functional material. The attractive potential of SMA includes its reversible strains of several percent, generation of high recovery stresses and the ability to lift a heavy weight.

Most industrial applications of SMA have been used for on/off applications, such as cooling circuit valves, fire detection systems, clamming devices.

SMA is very popular as an actuator, as the motor actuator can be reduced to a single SMA wire. The wire replaces all the complicated motor systems, is more compact and reliable and due to the absence of the electrical component, the shape memory actuator becomes a silent, friction-reduced and spark-free device.

Programming which allows specific movement to be designed can also create behaviours for controlling SMA.

Shape Memory Alloys have a lower Ni:Ti ratio so that they are martensitic at room temperature after cold drawing and heat treating for shape setting. After deformation, they will recover shape upon heating through the transformation of temperature. Their behaviour can be controlled through programming control and Arduino (Ng, 2014).

Workshop 11: Interactive Paper

Interactive Paper workshop utilises Bare Conductive paint. The paint provides a great platform for discovering, playing, repairing and designing with electronics.

You can use the paint for a range of applications, from creative to highly technical projects. The paint can be used as a liquid wire to draw or print graphical circuits, or even as a conductive adhesive

Technical Data: High Tech

Material Alchemy

eliminating the need for soldering equipment.

This makes it a great prototyping tool for makers of all ages. The paint also comes in handy for repairing electronics, such as PCBs, or even old TV remotes.

You can use the paint to create capacitive surfaces, so you can add interactivity onto almost any object. It can also be used alongside electrical components, prototyping materials, PCBs, microcontrollers, e-textiles, and conductive thread.

It is a nontoxic, solvent free, water soluble, air-drying paint that is child friendly, making it great for use at home or in the classroom

The paint works on many materials including paper, plastic, textiles and conventional electronics. Simply apply with a brush, roller, or screen print, leave to dry for 5 minutes, and start building interactive surfaces (Nelson, 2014).

CIRCUIT DIAGRAM

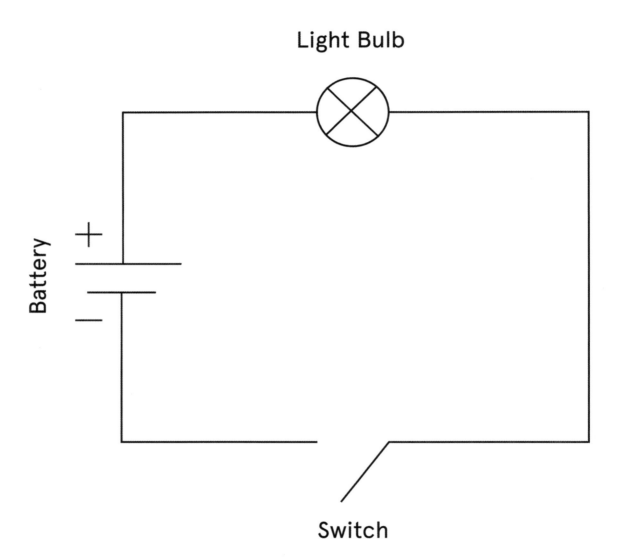

Technical Data: Squishy Circuits & Graphite Sounds

LAB SHEETS

TOUCH SENSITIVE DIAGRAM

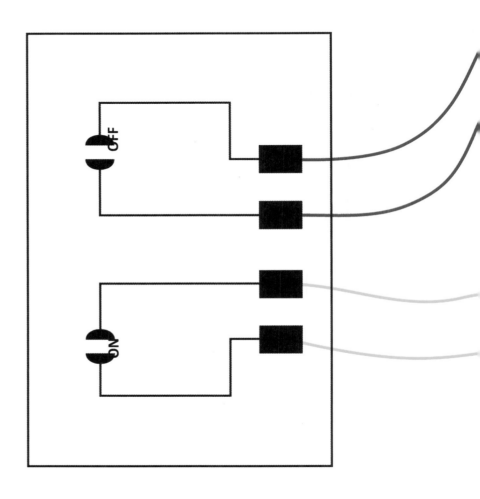

 0.27M ohm Resistor

330M ohm Resistor

 LED

Capacitor

Technical Data: Touch Sensitive

Material Alchemy

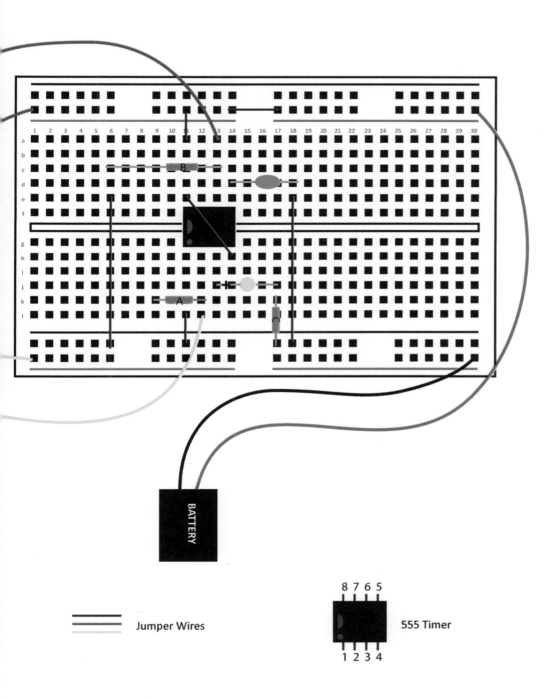

Jumper Wires

555 Timer

8 7 6 5

1 2 3 4

PRINT TEMPLATE

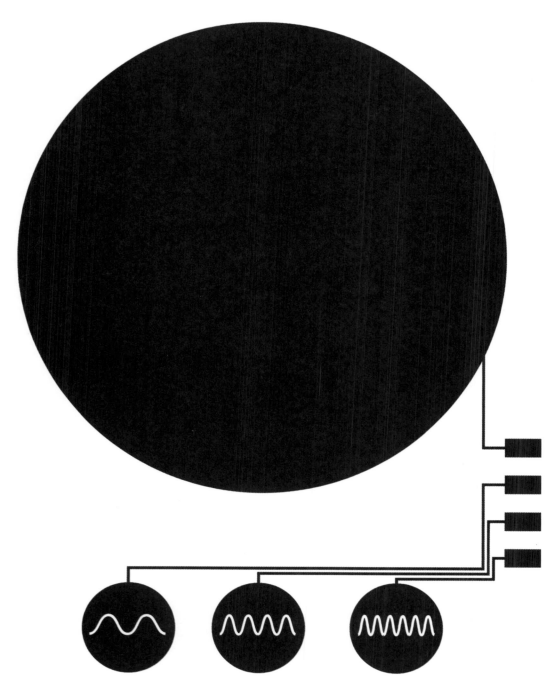

Technical Data: Interactive Paper

SENSOR DIAGRAM

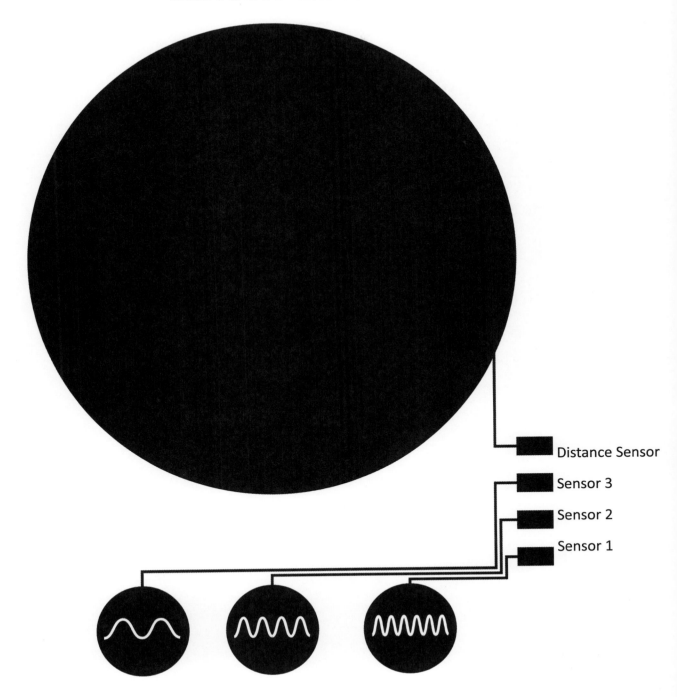

Image Credit: Image on opposite and current page created by Michael Shorter.

BULLDOG CLIP DIAGRAM

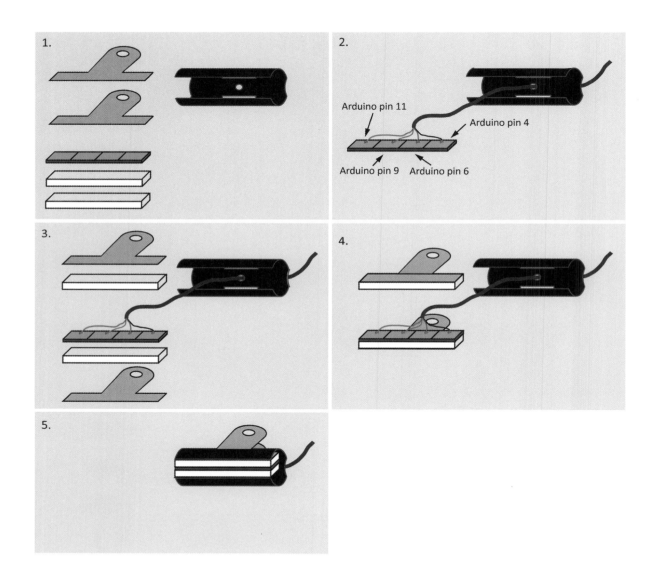

1.

2.
Arduino pin 11
Arduino pin 4
Arduino pin 9   Arduino pin 6

3.

4.

5.

Technical Data: Interactive Paper

ARDUINO DIAGRAM

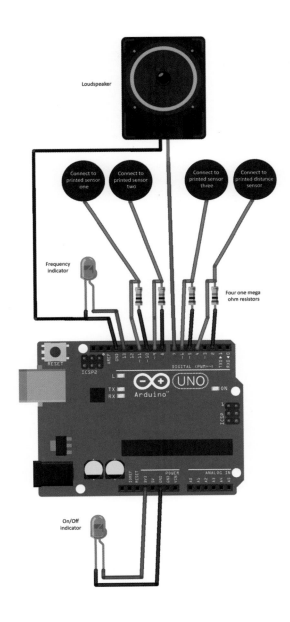

Image Credit: Image on opposite page created by Michael Shorter. Image on current page, created using Fritzing by Michael Shorter.

INTERACTIVE PAPER DIAGRAM

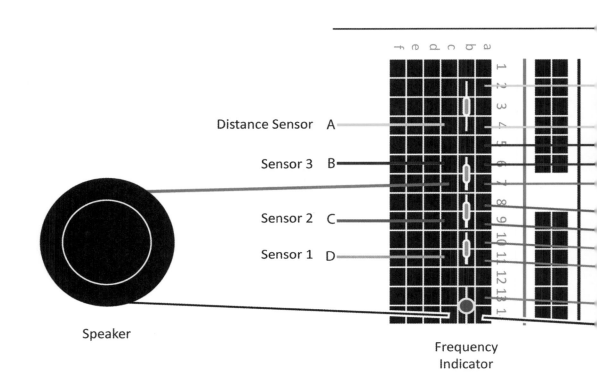

Distance Sensor A

Sensor 3 B

Sensor 2 C

Sensor 1 D

Speaker

Frequency
Indicator

Code

Wire 2, 4 and A	
Wire 5, 6 and B	
Wire 8, 9 and C	
Wire 10, 11 and D	
Wire 13	
Wire GND	
Resistor	
LED	

Technical Data: Interactive Paper

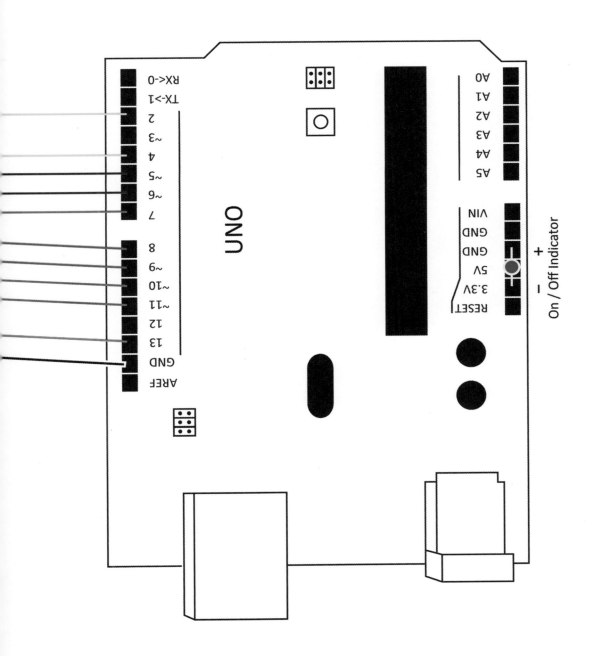

SMA DIAGRAM

SMA wire

Resistor

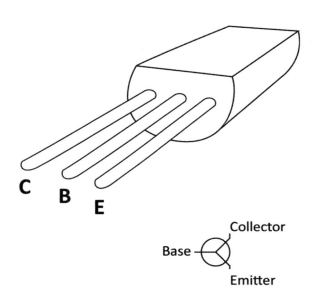

C B E

Collector

Base

Emitter

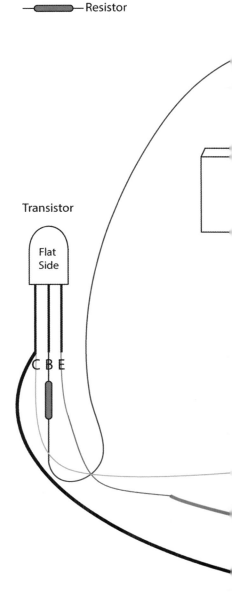

Transistor

Flat
Side

C B E

Technical Data: Tectonic Circuit

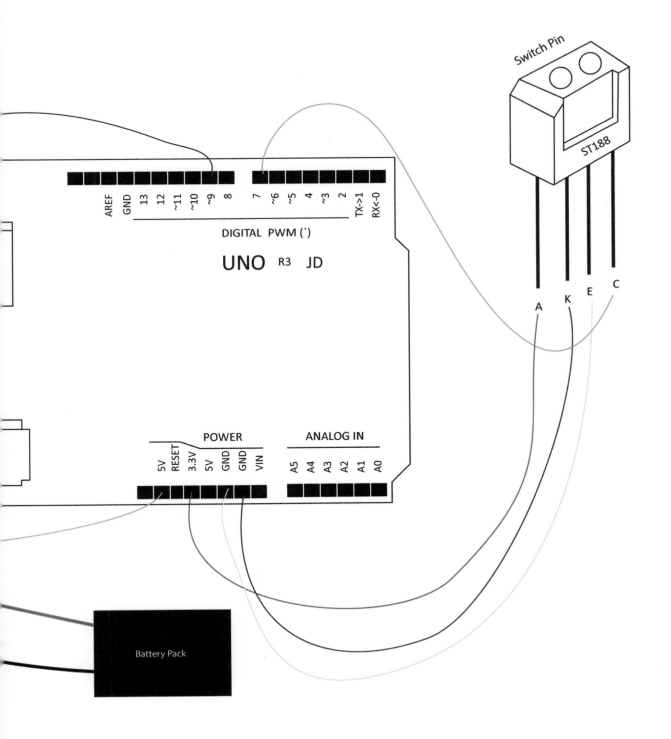

THE TEAM

Material Alchemy

[Publisher]
Rudolf Van Wezel
BIS Publisher

[Copy Editors]
Rowan Bailey
Clair Sweeney

[Interaction Producer]
Tom Forth &
imactivate Team

[Photographer & Stylist]
Studio Aikieu

[Technical]
Peter Kingsnorth
Daniel Loader

[Design Assistant]
Laura Elvira Martinez

[Animation Producer]
Josie Capel

[Foreword]
Philippa Wagner

[Material Forecasting]
Unique Style Platform

[Workshop Contributors]
Dr AnnMarie Thomas
The Playful Learning Lab
Bare Conductive
Berit Greinke
Miriam Ribul
Tamsyn Ainsworth
Andere Monjo
Laurence Humier
Laura Daza
The Fabrick Lab
Michael Shorter

[The Alchemists]
Sarah Linda Forrer
Studio Fludd
Clemens Winkler
Unfold
Jolan van der Wiel
Arabeschi di Latte
Ann-Kristin Abel
Formafantasma
Marjan van Aubel
Hyun Jin Jeong
Aagje Hoeskra
Adam Brown
Lucy McRae
Johanna Schmeer
The Kitchen

[Others]
Melissa Fletcher
Stephen Calcutt

VISIONARY

They have worked in partnership with Scientists, Technologists and Engineers, which have enabled the studio to provide fresh, innovative insights through the fabrication of thought-provoking outputs.

Working across all areas within the creative and business industry, Studio Aikieu has a keen interest and knowledge within the fields of science, technology, social anthropology and craftsmanship.

The hybrid approach of their practice is grounded in aesthetic sensibilities and inherent codes of human design, which have inspired the cultivation of original ideas that make tangible the most poignant of our social, ethical and environmental futures.

Through comprehensive research we are able to provide a range of services to suit your needs.

Studio Aikieu continuously tracks key innovations, trends and cultural developments that will impact design thinking across all disciplines.

Influenced by the principles of co-design, Studio Aikieu forges collaborative partnerships with key industry players, as they believe to find creative solutions, involves working with individuals and organisations from different fields.

The Vision: The Team

Material Alchemy

Visual Direction

We can help cultivate your organisation's visual direction through graphic styling, art direction and prop design, to craft engaging visual narratives which communicate the identity of your organisation's ethos and philosophy.

Concept Development

We have extensive knowledge about key global issues that shape our future environments and have worked in collaboration with various organisations to develop short, medium and long-term future concepts for commercial to high end industries.

Future Forecasting

Looking at both long and short-term trends that will influence the market, we provide you with a visual report, highlighting key drivers that will help you make vital strategic decisions that will shape the growth and development of your organisation.

Workshops

We run a series of workshops that help support organisations to think laterally, injecting some much needed innovation and fresh thinking. Workshops vary from material exploration, to ideas generation with a strong focus on colour and materials, digital applications, future thinking and creativity.

SERVICES

DIGITAL NARRATIVES

In 2013 Thomas Forth founded imactivate in Leeds, UK. Since then, the small team have been developing and refining technologies that let physical objects tell their stories in a digital world. One of their first creations is Rusty the Squeaky Robot; a lift-the-flap book for children of the 21st century. The product, is an ongoing collaboration with designer Neil Clark. Instead of extra content hiding behind flaps, the accompanying app unlocks additional sounds, games, translations and live readings that are digitally hidden on each page. Central to everything that imactivate do is a belief that physical objects and places have a story to tell. Their mission is to use the technology that surrounds us to unlock these stories in new and wonderful ways.

The Vision: The Team

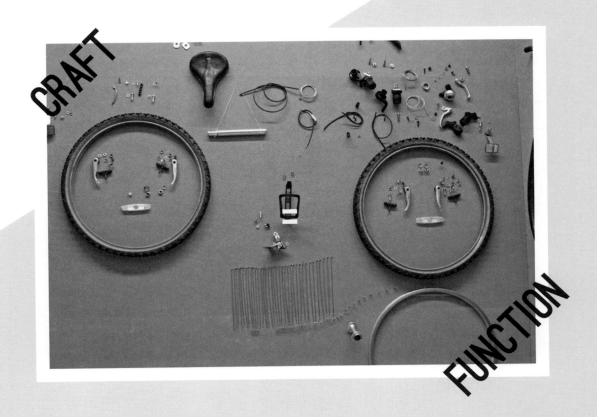

Josie Capel is a mixed media artist who explores the relationship between handcraftsmanship and digital manipulation. She mixes the tangible with the intangible to facilitate audience interactions and engagements with art. Craft=Function underpins Capel's practice. The driving factors of Capel's practice span a wide socio-political scope. The aim of these projects is to bring attention to topics which deserve the attention of an audience. The way she chooses to articulate this is through artistic intervention. Recent project investigations cover issues surrounding the diminishing cinema trade, dementia awareness, big data, technological dependence, homelessness, and cycling safety.

FUTURE GAZERS

through daily blog posts, as well as working with our in-house design teams at strategic points through the season. USP's team of leading trend experts – from colour and materials, to fashion, retail and consumer insight – works with leading brands in categories including FMCG, beauty, fashion and healthcare. The creative team is headed up by founder Jane Kellock with Jo Shiers, Gwyneth Holland and Philippa Wagner, supported by a global network of trend experts, creatives, makers and style influencers.

Unique Style Platform (USP) is a trend service that offers intelligent analysis to the fashion & lifestyle industries. USP specialises in tangible, inspirational trends that help creative teams to understand seasonal design and product directions, as well as the future world of their consumer. USP supports the way creatives now find inspiration - in both physical and digital ways. The team freely shares its ideas

The Vision: The Team

Laura Martinez is a Spanish researcher and multidisciplinary designer based in London. Martinez's work explores the boundaries between digital technologies and craftsmanship, questioning how traditional craft techniques can be implemented and combined with digital processes. With over ten years experience working in the areas of fashion, art and textiles, she specialises in technology and material research for surface design.

Her most recent project Digicrafted challenges the undefined parameter where traditional textiles and additive technologies are combined to craft a new digital aesthetic. Her work has been widely showcased at various prestigious venues such as Audax Textile Museum in Tilburg, the V2_ Institute for the Unstable Media in Rotterdam and CSM Innovation Centre, among others. More recently, she has exhibited for the British Council at Beirut Design Week and the London, Paris and New York editions of 3D Printshow.

ATELIER

DIGITAL NOMAD

Stephen Calcutt is a Digital Nomad, intrigued by all things tech, continuously tinkering with found objects, questioning the role and impact of technology within society. Calcutt works in the field of interactive technologies. Calcutt's research interests lie in the development of interactive, kinetic and robotic sculpture and he is particularly interested in how viewers perceive artworks that perform tasks, based around data and its visualisation. His kinetic sculpture, Internet Wind (an installation that investigates audience engagements with simulations of telepresence) was nominated for the Axis MA Star Award 2010. He has exhibited widely at events such as the Abandon Normal Devices Festival and the International Triennial in Istanbul.

The Vision: The Team

Material Alchemy

Melissa Fletcher is a couturist, who is interested in exploring emerging technologies. She is currently experimenting with the digital Amaya to challenge its use from a traditional crafts perspective. Inspired by the emerging trend 'Man vs Machine', she is interested in how we can utilise new technologies

SLOW CRAFT

to craft the human touch. Fletcher's research lies in the production of bespoke luxury. She is driven by aesthetic sensibilities and codes inherent within textiles. She is particularly interested in 'slow luxury' and how, within a digitalised society, we often turn to stitch as a means for reflective contemplation.

A
Antichit Belsito
www.antichitabelsito.it

Arduino
www.arduino.cc

Ada Fruit
www.adafruit.com

B
Bare Conductive
www.bareconductive.com

Better Equipped
www.betterequipped.co.uk

C
ColourCraft
www.colourcraft.com

Cass Art
www.cassart.co.uk

E
El Wire Craft
www.elwirecraft.co.uk

Educational Innovations
www.teachersource.com

F
Fred Aldous
www.fredaldous.co.uk

Fabrick Lab
www.thefabricklab.com

G
Grand Illusions
www.grand-illusions.com

Glow Wire

www.glowire.com

Good Fellow
www.goodfellow.com

H
Hindleys
www.hindleys.com

I
Inventables
www.inventables.com

K
Kitronik
www.kitronik.co.uk

L
L'Cornellissen
www.cornelissen.com

London Graphic Centre
www.londongraphics.co.uk

M
Mindsetonline
www.mindsetsonline.co.uk

Mansolar
www.mansolar.com

Modulor
www.modulor.de

Makers Shed
www.makershed.com

N
Neon String
www.neonstring.com

O
Oomlout

www.oomlout.co.uk

P
Plug and Wear
www.plugandwear.com

Power Magnetic Store
www.powermagnetstore.com

S
Squishy Circuit
www.squishycircuitsstore.com

Spark Fun
www.sparkfun.com

Sugru
www.sugru.com

T
Tim Star
www.timstar.co.uk

The Engineer Guy
www.theengineerguy.com

Resources: Suppliers & Material Organisations

Material Alchemy

A
Advanced Material Research Institute
www.amri.uno.edu

A to Z of Materials
www.azom.com

Architerials
www.architerials.com

Arduino
www.arduino.cc

C
Centre for Materials Research
www.cmr.qmul.ac.uk

Cereplast
www.cereplast.com

D
Design Research Lab
www.design-research-lab.org

E
Environmental Design Research Society
www.edra.org

Electric Foxy
www.electricfoxy.com

Everywhere Tech
www.everywheretech.org

H
High Low Tech
www.highlowtech.org

I
Ingredients
www.moreingredients.com

Institute of Materials, Minerals & Mining
www.iom3.org

Institute of Making
www.materialslibrary.org.uk

Institute of Material Research
www.engineering.leeds.ac.uk/imr/

L
Little Bits
www.littlebits.cc

Lithuanian Materials Research
www.ltmrs.lt

Library of 3D Molecular Structures
www.nyu.edu

M
Material Lab
www.material-lab.co.uk
MIT Media Lab
www.media.mit.edu

Material Sense
www.materialsense.com

Materia
www.materia.nl

Material Research Society
www.nanohub.org

Materiability
www.materiability.com

N
Next Nature

www.nextnature.net

O
Open Materials
www.openmaterials.org

P
Philips Design
www.design.philips.com/probes

R
Royal Society of Chemisty
www.chemsoc.org

Rematerialise Project
www.kingston.ac.uk

S
Surface Thinking
www.surfacethinking1.blogspot.com

T
Transmaterial
www.transmaterial.net

The Interactive Institute
www.tii.se

Textile Futures Research Centre
www.tfrc.org.uk

U
University of St Thomas
www.stthomas.edu

UCL
www.ucl.ac.uk/cmr

W
Wearable Senses
www.wearablesenses.net

B
Braddock-Clarke, S & Mahony, M (2007). Techno Textiles 2: Revolutionary Fabrics for Fashion and Design. Thames & Hudson: UK.

Bradley, Q (2011). Design Futures. Merrell Publishers: UK.

Bradley, Q (2012). Fashion Futures. Merrell Publishers: UK.

C
Casey- Reas, C (2010). Form+Code in Design, Art, and Architecture. Princeton Architectural Press: USA.

Cobb, V. (1994). Science Experiments You Can Eat. Revised Edition. Harper Collins: New York.

D
Dunne, A & Raby, F. (2014). Speculative Everything: Design, Fiction, and Social Dreaming. MIT Press: USA.

E
Eng, D. (2009) Fashion Geek. North Lights: New York.

H
Humier, L. (2012) Cooking Material. Triennale Design Museum: Italy.

Hartman, K. (2013) Make: Wearable. Maker Media: CA.

Howes, P. (2012) Material Matters. Blackdog Publishers: UK.

K
Karana, E. (2013). Materials Experience: Fundamentals of Materials and Design. Butterworth-Heinemann: UK.

Klanten, R. (2011). A Touch of Code: Interactive Installations and Experiences. Die Gestalten Verlag: Berlin.

L
Lee, S & Du Preez, W. (2007). Fashioning the Future: Tomorrow's Wardrobe. Thames & Hudson: London.

Lewis, A. (2008) Switch Craft. Potter Craft: NY.

Lewis, P. (2012). Material World: The Modern Craft Bible. Virgin Books: UK.

Lefteri, C. (2014) Materials for Design. Laurence King: UK.

Lefteri, C. (2006) Materials for Inspiration. Rotavision: UK.

Light-Brown, C (2008) Amazing Kitchen Chemistry Projects You can Build Yourself. Nomad Press: USA.

M
Mahony, M (2011). Advanced Textiles for Health and Wellbeing. Thames & Hudson: UK.

Miodownik, M. (2013). Stuff Matters: The Strange Stories of the Marvellous Materials that Shape Our Man-made World. Viking: USA.

Myers, W. (2012). BioDesign. Thames&Hudson: UK.

O
Olsson, T. (2012) Arduino Wearables. Apress: New York.

P
Pakhchyan, S. (2008) Fashioning Technology. O'Reilly Media: USA.

Q
Quellen Field, S. (2011) Culinary Reactions: The Everyday Chemistry of Cooking. Chicago Review Press: USA.

Quinn, B. (2010) Textile Futures. Bloomsbury Publishing: UK.

R
Ritter, A (2006). Smart Materials in Architecture, Interior Architecture and Design: Types, Products, Architecture. Birkhäuser GmbH: Berlin.

S
Seymour, S (2009). Fashionable Technology: The Intersection of Design, Fashion, Science and Technology. Springer: New York.

T
This, H (2008). Molecular Gastronomy Exploring the Science of Flavor. Columbia University Press: New York.

Resources: Books & Alchemists